MW00640072

From Hard To Heart

By Carrie Bryant

The Great House Publishing (NBN) Inc.

From Hard to Heart®
Copyright © 1999 by Pastor/Presiding Elder Carrie Bryant. All rights reserved. Published in 1999. Printed In the United States of America

ISBN 1-889448-53-2 (hard)
Published by The Great House Publishing (NBN) Inc.
P.O. Box 574244
Orlando, Florida
32857
Requests for information should be addressed to the above address:

Library of Congress Cataloguing-in-Publication Data
From Hard to Heart: Autobiography written by Carrie Bryant
                        Compiled & co-written by Joan Mattison Daniel
                        & Winfred Bowers Henry
Library of Congress Catalog Card Number: **98-091112**
Bryant, Carrie

From Hard to Heart: Autobiography of the life of Pastor/Presiding
                        Elder Carrie Bryant Founder & Pastor of
                        Tabernacle Churches in certain Regions of the
                        State Of Florida & of other churches birth from
                        the ministry. This work chronicles A 'True Rags
                        to Riches Success Story', of a life that was good as
                        dead. It Tells of her survival, the powerful Works
                        of God in her lifetime.

Unless otherwise indicated, all Old and New Testament scripture references are taken from The Holy Bible: King James Version.

Book Design by GP Design Dot USA
Cover design by Ivy Lee & Stephanie Musser

GREAT HOUSE PUBLISHING (NBN) INC.
Orlando. Toronto. New York

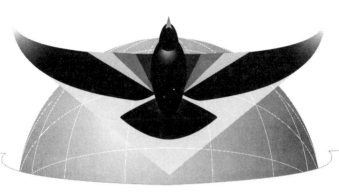

THE GREAT HOUSE PUBLISHING (NBN) INC.

©

TABLE OF CONTENTS

PART I
Separating the Clay - The Outside World

PART II
Death of My First Husband - Churches Birthed from Ministry

INTRODUCTION
Destined to leadership God's Way

There are times, perhaps that you have prayed and prayed about a situation, and the answer just never comes. The answer is there but sometimes delayed. God uses many situations to mold us, and some situations are for His glory. From Hard to Heart is a warm provoking book in the sense to inspire you to hold on, to continue in righteousness and to encourage you to blossom in the call that God has ordained for your life.

Through the drudgery of my early life, I always wanted to be a model for God not cognizant of what it took to be God's model. However, as I look back over the pattern of my life, I recognized I was destined to leadership, God's way.

Most of us have at least one memory that stands out in our lives. Unfortunately, in my case there are many - from the red-clay hills of Georgia to the sunny flat land of Florida. Sometimes it's impossible to distinguish from my direct memories or memories that were rehearsed by others; however, they are there.

Having been torn away from my family at the age of three years old, to be given away by my biological father while my mother was at work is one embedded memory that impacted my life. I constantly wondered, Lord, Why me? Now, I know it was in God's plan for my life. We all have a path we must follow, some a little more rugged than others. Regardless, our lives are pre-destined.

Through all the hurts, heartaches, pain and sufferings, I emerged a model for God. He molded and shaped me into what I am today. I have now come to terms with the pattern of my life to know it was God's plan for me.

As my life unfolds on paper, I pray that it will be a beacon of light for someone in darkness. A source of hope for the discouraged; a mustard seed of faith for the hopeless; joy to the sorrowful; healing for the battered; peace for the confused; strength for the weak, and steadfastness for the wavering. God had control of my life from conception.

I also pray that each leader whom the Lord is calling to a higher calling find encouragement and to firmly grip the solid rock who is Jesus after reading From Hard to Heart.

DEDICATED TO:

My children

James and Elizabeth
Carsandra
Kevin and Tisha

My grandchildren

Shakeen
Adonnis

ACKNOWLEDGEMENTS

Most autobiographies have been written by more than one person. I'm sure I am not alone when I say I owe much gratitude to the ones who helped me get this piece of work on paper. I want to express my gratitude to my secretaries for encouraging me to share my life story with others. My thanks to Prophet Michael Lattibeaudeaire for his patience and help in making this book become a reality. I acknowledge my members and friends who played a part in this project.

Special thanks go to Joan Daniel and Winifred Henry, my writers, who have given so generously of their time, efforts and patience. For they have been a source of strength as I recalled some painful memories while putting this book together. My thanks go to my family for their support.

GRATITUDE TO THE DAUGHTER OF INHERITANCE AND THE SON OF ENCOURAGEMENT

With much gratitude to the "Daughter of Inheritance" and our personal "Son of encouragement", Deacon Ronald Nathan and his wife Sister Ingrid Nathan, both ministers of music at the church. A special thank you goes out to this young couple for their willingness and obedience to the voice of the Lord. Without the sacrifice of this couple, the Sanford Tabernacle of Prayer would not have the dwelling place it now possesses in Sanford, FL. I am eternally grateful that they extended the gift of love; Ingrid, donating the land inherited to her for the up building of God's Kingdom. The most amazing part of this act of kindness is they had no credentials about me, a total stranger to them. It must have been the spirit of God in my life that they could identify with. Through your generosity God would not allow your kind deed to go without rewarded. My blessings to you and your family as you enter your new home (right next to mine). Your labor was not in vain in the Lord. Son and daughter, I love and appreciate your family and all the sacrifices you have made.

Eternally Grateful,

Pastor Carrie B. Bryant

A NOTE OF APPRECIATION
By Dr. Faye Carson

I Thess. 5:11, "Wherefore comfort yourselves together, and edify one another, even as also ye do."

Down through the years Pastor Carrie Buie Bryant has been a blessing to my life. As a member of the Tabernacle of Prayer in Brooklyn, New York, I remember sitting in anticipation of what God would say through her from the first time that she ministered. It was Pastor Bryant who God used to warn us of an impending shaking of the Tabernacle of Prayer prior to the death of our founder, Pastor Johnnie Washington. At that time, Pastor assured us that the prophecy was of the Lord, and he would not be here to help us when the shaking took place.

In June of 1988, a group of teachers of the Tabernacle Bible Institute and others came to Sanford to participate in a graduation exercise. We were able to stay for Sunday service. During the service, we began to pull on the Pastor's spirit in such a way that she called me into her office and told me that she would be coming to the hotel after service to minister to us. Pastor Bryant came to our hotel.

There was a group of eight people gathered in the room. I remember one saint, Sis. Eileen Johnson was ministered to regarding her situation. I was able to see everything that Pastor spoke come to pass in Eileen's life. She ministered to Sis. Betty Warren. She told her that God said she was resting in His bosom. Since that time, God has proven to Sis. Warren that she holds a special place in Him.

Next pastor Bryant ministered to me. I was told that God had given me the ability to love people, and that he was going to send people to me. My instructions were to love them with the love that God had placed in my heart. God further promised that He would replace the love that I would give away with His love. From that time to this, God has sent people from all walks of life for me to love. And, as He promised, each time I have given love without measure, God has replaced that love with His love.

The Lord has used Pastor Bryant to bring words of encouragement to me in my home on a number of occasions. Each time was when I was desperate to hear from the Lord. Each message was custom designed for my situation.

In February of 1997, Pastor Bryant again ministered to me. Prior to coming to Florida, there was a question in my heart regarding my place in ministry. I wanted to be sure that I was hearing from the Lord and that I was following in His footsteps. It seemed to me that God might be speaking to my heart telling me that it was time to make a move. I had even gone to investigate another church. But, when I got to Florida, as Pastor Bryant was ministering, God sent her to me with a message. I was told that God had placed me in this ministry and that I was to stay in place because I was a survivor. I received an assurance that caused me to know that this was the time to stand still and remain steadfast in ministry.

Finally, this year, when I needed to be encouraged, Pastor Bryant had her dean, Dean Joan Daniel to call me and ask that I come to Sanford and be graduation speaker. In the beginning the date prevented me from agreeing to come, but Pastor was persistent and changed the date. This was a most blessed weekend. It was the refreshing that I needed to provide strength to continue doing His will.

PREFACE

Men have historically used the judgments at the Garden of Eden rendered on Eve [the female side of Man] whom the Lord God had made to govern and administrate His Kingdom on the earth. As a result of the transgression, they have used the sentence as a weapon to govern and control, dominate and subjugate the lives of their fellowmen, especially women. They failed to recognized and became blind to the 'Original Commission', which gave all men the right to govern all things but not the right and power to dominate another man's life, in this case the lives of women.

Since the fall of man we have all experienced and seen this dominance displayed before our very eyes, restraint only by the grace and love of Almighty God. Man's government and equally the barbarism of our so-called 'civilized societies' have handed down to us generations of pain and sufferings, with the exception of a few good reigns throughout the ages.

On the contrary, Jesus Christ, Himself alone, as God incarnate, established and classically displayed a different heavenly pattern filled with a divine standard. In his days man's religious order filled with the arrogance and hypocrisy of the likes of the Pharisees, Sadducees, Scribes, Zealots, Doctors, Lawyers, coupled with the dominance of Hellenism and the blindness of the Roman Empire held women prisoners. Especially, those responsible for the law who taught 'males' to pray such prayers as, 'I thank you Lord that I was not born a woman' coupled with their segregated places of worship which encouraged ignorance and the imprisonment of women by fear and condemnation.

Jesus Christ on the other hand personally motivated encouraged and inspired women to reach for their highest potential and to live out their God-ordained destiny. He visited them, sanctified their faith and gave all equal attention. Jesus was and is the 'Greatest Liberator Of Women' the world has ever and will ever see. Throughout the ages He has freed their spirits, encouraged their souls, healed their bodies and possessed their being through the sweetness of His Holy Spirit. Thus, women passed through the way of the cross and have been raised to a much higher spiritual order, for so it is written, "He has raised us up together and caused us to be seated in heavenly places in Christ Jesus".

In the Western world and the development of American societies, women passed through the same darkness of the Dark Ages and the development of the American Nation, as anyone of our generation. Righteous and evil women vied for their place in such societies some to insanity, corruption, and destruction and others to the rewards of righteousness and wisdom.

With the emergence of the Anti-slavery movements, there also arose the Woman's Suffrage Movement, which includes the likes of Sojourner Truth, Harriet Tubman, Susan B. Anthony and many other notable women. During those movements great men like William J. Seymour and Bishop C. H. Mason included 'the dual-sex government', notable for its African heritage in the development of their religious movements. The African-American Community has long been the heartthrob of this 'dual-sex regime'. It had long embraced this 'Christ-like form of leadership' which advocates 'In Christ there is neither male nor female'. This form of leadership had received its dynamic thrust from the foundation of Christ's model, which can clearly be seen throughout the New Testament, including the Pentecostal revival of A.D. 30, in Jerusalem.

In this form of leadership, they also encouraged women to reach for their highest goals and fulfillment of their God ordained destiny. This form of equality was already self-evident in the African-American community, so richly preserved throughout by the rigor of the wretchedness of slavery. Thus, during the Civil Rights Movements, women served in command on the issues of woman and family. Therefore, the role of the African-American woman in all of these movements and her community was self-evident, where she starred passionately beside her counterpart and was success under the inspiration, motivation and encouragement from the Presence of the Lord.

Pastor Bryant, likewise was a pioneer and forerunner of her time, who went on this campaign of the Lord. At the time when women were denied access to the pulpit of the church of the Lord Jesus, in certain parts of the African-American Community, she, as a woman, went on the warpath for Jesus for equal and open access to minister the word of the Lord. She like many other women went on this warpath through 'Strict Obedience to the Voice of the Lord'. This reality was strikingly real as it put her on the point of the spear, with the adversary on the opposing point. She had never felt that her battle was against flesh and blood, nor one of male against female, but throughout her long service to Christ, she believed 'this was a spiritual battle'.

During her times, when God had called her to the ministry, many of the men whom God was calling were out of position and place, unable to answer the divine call. She has always felt and often taught her congregations that Eve, the woman had gotten the man, Adam into trouble, through the transgression. Therefore, she felt that the woman as a whole must once again rally to the call and help get the man back into his rightful position.

But when she arrived on the public scene, 'crying loud and sparing not', she met ruthless oppositions. These oppositions were largely from the male dominant pulpit of the Black Churches; so ruthless were these oppositions that underground circulation was sent to many churches to refrain from accepting her in their churche's. Those who accepted her used her as a drawing card, a main attraction for financial gain.

Nevertheless, Pastor Bryant like many other successful women weathered the storms and escaped to tell the story, as she so often has said, "I am one who escaped to tell the story". She is a real rags to riches story, and has become a part of the company of 'those divinely harvested women', that God harvested between the sixties and the eighties for the twenty-first century. This autobiography should prove a wonderful tell-story that will inspire many to fulfill their God ordained destiny.

-Michael Liberte Lattibeaudeaire

CHAPTER ONE

Part 1

SEPARATING THE CLAY

*"Looking Back I Can See
How the Potter Began
To Separate the Clay
That Would Later Be
Molded Into the Chosen Vessel."*

It was in the fall of 1939, on the 3rd day of September, the leaves had begun to turn their colors and fall from the trees. The time had come for Rosa Watson-Hunt to give birth to Carrie Denyce. I was the fifth of six children born to Lester and Rosa Lee Hunt. The little town of Dublin was a bleak and red clay country-side. During this time, births were held in homes assisted by mid-wives. Reflecting back my mother was only sixteen years old when she married my father, who was the son of Rufus and Hattie Hunt. Daddy was seven years her senior. He along with his older brother Odabe[pronounced as Oda B.,] and sister, Oradessa were reared by their grandparents Reverend Wally and Tobitha Wells, who were sharecroppers. Lester's mother died a tragic death. While giving birth to her fourth child, she died along with the child. Lester lived most of his young life in the country of Dublin, Georgia.

Rosa Lee Watson, my mother, was the daughter of a Cherokee Indian, Yank Watson. I was named after my maternal grandmother, Carrie Watson. After the birth of five girls and one boy her father moved with his tribe. They moved out of the state of Georgia and all contact was lost. Grandmother Carrie and her six children lived their lives as best they could in the city of Dublin, Georgia.

Daddy's health was poor, and he had an addiction to alcohol. This was common among many young men in those days. The bottle appeared to be the savior, to drive out whatever was ailing the person. In addition to this problem, life's everyday toils brought about added stress to the marriage. A child (Willie Mae) was born outside this union between the second and third child, Jeanelle and Lester, Jr.

The family lived in the country, but at the time of each delivery my mother, nicknamed "Candy", would travel to the city to be with my grandmother to give birth and receive much needed help with the baby. It is speculated that during this time, Willie Mae was born.

We were all born one or two years apart. There were two other children to be born into the family before mother moved to the city permanently. After I was born there was no more commuting between births.

The Hunt family moved to the City of Dublin, away from the country. Daddy was unable to work and his habit at the time seemed uncontrollable; this led my mother to seek work in Brunswick, GA. She now had my baby brother Herbert. Mother's life appeared to have crumbled due to her husband's health and lifestyle, not to mention six small children to care for which seemed insurmountably hopeless. She continued to work in Brunswick, commuting back and forth to Dublin where there were more job opportunities and better pay. She did her best to provide for us.

Now we were able to move into a house with four rooms. The house was nicer than what we had, with better floors and a roof that would endure rain and strong winds. The house consisted of a living room, one bedroom, kitchen, and bathroom. Later our dad came and joined the family. Mother would leave on Monday and would return Friday night or early Saturday morning. It depended on how long it took her to complete the work done in Brunswick. My older siblings cared for us younger ones as best they could with the help of our dad and grandmother. Our move now placed us just two blocks away from our Grandmother Carrie.

There were many difficult days ahead; some came sooner than ever anticipated. Who would have imagined the difficult days would begin with me? I can't quite recall all of the events, but some stand out far clearer than others do. I could not remember many of these events; some were retold to me by my older siblings and father.

It was Christmas time. My father's aunt would come by to visit us at least once a year. This was a joyous occasion because she would bring many items the family needed. We weren't able to afford much, but we were happy; we had each other. She would come to bring us toys, food, clothes, money, and other things our parents weren't able to purchase or obtain.

This particular trip, Mom was out of town working as she so often did. I was left home with my siblings and dad. My mother always took Herbert with her; he was too little to be left with us. My great aunt saw me, and her heart went out to this little girl with a runny nose, tangled black silky hair, wearing hand me-downs. She wanted to know where my mother was. Dad replied, "She's gone." I don't know if she thought my dad meant she just left us with him never to return or what. He didn't explain the situation to her. Aunt Maggie said, "Lester, you should give me this little girl". Dad being filled with his joy juice at the time said, "You can have her; shucks take 'em all". At this time I wondered what made me so special. I guess my older sisters and brothers could relate to the puppy in the pound being taken first over the older dogs. Or I can imagine how foster children may feel when they have visitors, and they only want to see the babies and small children. At this time I was about three years old. Well, the chain of events began to happen.

CHAPTER TWO

THE BEGINNING OF A NEW LIFE

My father consented to my Aunt Maggie's taking me home with her. Before the journey began my sister Jeanelle proceeded to wash me, preparing me for my new home. This was a moment I will never forget. The foot tub (basin) was filled with water from the pump outside. Jeanelle lifted me up to the table and began to first wash my face with the washrag; you may call it a cloth, but it was a rag. Tears began to stream down my face. I cried continuously. I remember my sister telling me to stop crying. She said, "I wish it could be me". Those words didn't stop the tears from flowing. She tried to comfort me. She began to undo my worn braids and brush my hair. It was shoulder length, jet black, and curly. At

23

each stroke I could only imagine this would be the last time my sister would do my hair. As I think of it on today's terms, I was being divorced from my family.

As my sister finished washing me she began to dress me. My dad and Aunt Maggie along with the rest of my sisters and brothers waited out on the porch. The sniffles could be heard through the tattered screen door. Jeanelle had a bag with some of my belongings in her hand. They were handed to my aunt. I remember them telling me to stop crying, but nothing said or done could stop the tears. I felt I had left part of my life behind me as I left my two sisters, two brothers and Daddy waving good-bye from the porch steps. Jeanelle had my hair parted down the middle with two plaits, one on each side. I walked up to the car and was lifted onto the back seat by my sister and was given a kiss. "You'll love it there in *'Plorida'*". I cried the distance from home to the next stop.

My mother never found out about this scenario until she returned on Friday night. She would hear of this upon her arrival from a hard week's work and long commute from Brunswick with my brother Herbert. She returned home to her family minus her baby girl, Carrie. She was heartbroken. She couldn't believe her husband could give her baby girl away, although the help was needed and after all, this was family. Nothing she could do, so she consented.

The next stop was the city of Dublin. We pulled up to a store. It wasn't until the tears were dried up that I saw people of the other race. For in the country, we only saw people who looked like us. We went to the back of the store and waited our turn to be served. It appeared to me that this man knew my daddy's aunt. At this stop, my aunt purchased clothes, shoes, toys, a coat and all the accessories needed for me to begin a new life befitting to her standard of living. At this time my little bag was no longer needed. I thought I had moved from "Rags to Riches".

However things purchased brought about a little excitement, but this only held back the tears temporarily. My eyes filled with water again. I may have looked like a princess on the outside, but the void still remained. I could only think of my abrupt departure that tore me away from my family.

When we got to the country we spent the night at Aunt Oradessa's house. I remember asking Aunt Maggie, "When are we going to get to *'Plorida'*?" This night must have been one of the longest nights of my life. I cried myself to sleep.

The next morning we left Dublin and made several stops before entering the City of Sanford, Florida. This would be the place of my new residence. It wasn't until we drove into the driveway of her home that I found things so impressive of this great place of Plorida that had been mentioned in my hearing so often. My eyes lit up and I made this statement in a tiny child-like voice, "We made it to *'Plorida'*!"

All my tears vanished after seeing this huge, White House with a porch that appeared to encircle the entire house. The flowers were in full bloom, and orange trees stood tall with oranges dangling from them so beautifully. This scenery captured all sorrow and was replaced with a peace and joy words could not express. I felt like the little princess now both inside and out. Now I definitely thought I had made it from "Rags to Riches". Looking back I can see how the potter began to **Separate The Clay** that would later be molded into the chosen vessel.

CHAPTER THREE

MY NEW FAMILY

After seeing my new house in its splendor, I jumped out of the car with excitement. I hadn't done much traveling while in Dublin. This place I was taken to left me breathless. For I had never seen a house so big. I began walking up the stairs taking one tiny step at a time. I didn't say much. This lady who took me away from my dwelling and now to replace my mother was still a stranger to me. Although she had taken me shopping and bought me things I didn't even know existed, it was all still new to me. As my aunt began to turn the knob, there was a surprise there for me. Little did I know standing behind the door was the greatest thrill of all. The first person to greet us was my Uncle Will (who I later called Dad).

When we laid eyes upon each other, it was love at first sight. He was the same height as my dad, dressed in khaki dungarees and shirt, clean shaven, and very soft-spoken. His first words were, "Who do we have here?" I just stood staring at his face. His voice was very soft compared to my dad's deep baritone pitch. He got no response, so he scooped me up in his arms and embraced me. For some unknown reason I felt relaxed in his presence.

He and my Aunt had been married many years, but were unable to bear children. My Aunt informed him that her nephew, Lester, had given them this "'lil girl". This was his first acknowledgment of the addition to the family due to lack of the invention of a quicker way to inform him of the news. There were no complaints from my Uncle. I didn't know I had brought such joy to his life after my arrival. Having seen him only for a few seconds I felt a peace and a feeling of belonging. It appeared that our spirits immediately bonded.

We entered the house and the first thing I can remember seeing was this house filled with the nicest furniture I had ever seen. There were hardwood floors that you could see your reflection on. Each little step I took I could see my black patent leather shoes, white-laced socks, and pretty white lace from my slip underneath my dress fanning out about six inches around my torso. I guess I looked like the dolls I saw on the coffee table. The only difference was that I was real not made of porcelain and our colors weren't the same. The dolls were accompanied by other porcelain objects such as bells, statuettes, picture frames of people I wasn't familiar with, a crystal candy dish, and other whatnots, all resting on a white eyelet linen cloth. The house was so clean that it appeared to shine.

The house I came from was tidy, but nothing to be compared to this. There was an icebox in the other corner of the house and adjacent to it was a table that seated six. This was so new to me I must have forgotten about my aunt and uncle's presence.

Uncle Will was a mild, quiet man with a big heart. He was a deacon of the church and very faithful to his stewardship. Uncle Will worked in Sanford as a laborer. Sanford was a small town and the work was seasonal. Aunt Maggie was a deaconess and a missionary of the church. She would work right along with my uncle faithfully. She was very active with the youth. Any facet of operations, you could find her fulfilling the scripture, Ecclesiastics 9:10 "Whatsoever thy hand findeth to do, do it with thy might; for there is no work, nor device, nor knowledge, nor wisdom, in the grave whither thou goest." She served on the Usher Board, Pastor's Aide, Choir, Ladies Auxiliary, Church Clerk; you name it she would be found doing something to help.

They were both very active and dedicated to the church. As a matter of fact I think this was the first trip we took after settling in my new home, "the church". After I had finished my tour of the living room and dining area, we all prepared to go to church. This was the beginning of my spiritual background. The foundation was now being laid. I had heard my Grandmother Carrie talk about the Lord quite frequently. Now I would begin to have more visits to the place of which she so often spoke.

I was always very observant of my surroundings. When I first arrived at the church, I saw this wood framed structure. The grounds were neatly kept, and people were embracing one another as they met. You would think they had not seen each other from one holiday to the next. I soon realized this is according to scripture. It also made you feel loved.

Upon entering the church there were wooden pews, a bass drum, scrub board, and tambourines. The instrument that fascinated me the most was the piano. I fell in love with the sound of that big instrument. As I look back now I continue to see how God had his hand on me at a very early age.

At the early stages of my arrival, I remember being in the back seat of the Model T Ford to pick up the Mothers of the church and other members. We were one of the first families to have a car and did most of the transporting of the saints to and from the church. Many times my uncle, whom I now called Dad would drop off one load and pick up the next group. Very seldom did I miss a trip. Whenever the car cranked up, I expected to be a passenger. I hadn't been around long before the people began to ask where this little girl came from. My bright eyes and glowing smile would later become my trademark. This soon brought about many free ice cream cones and lollipops.

I began to meet more family members who would later have a great impact on my spiritual life. The "Black Family" was close to me because my cousin, Nina would become my baby-sitter, and the Black children took on the role of my brothers and sisters. Cousin Nina had moved from Georgia to live with Aunt Maggie in Florida much earlier before I came. She got married out of her home and had now started a family of her own. Aunt Maggie was considered the "Moses" of the family. She was the reason many of her brothers and sisters and their children moved from Dublin (country) to Sanford (city life). Because of her lifestyle, Cousin Nina, and her husband, Israel had given their lives to the Lord. They too had become very faithful members of the church.

Another one of Aunt Maggie's nieces, Nettie, had moved from Georgia to Florida. They (Nina and Nettie) were only six months apart and appeared inseparable. She too later married right out of Aunt Maggie's home. She also received salvation after spending time with her aunt, and she became very active in the church also. The family members worshiped at the same church. Aunt Maggie was the drawing card to many family members' salvation.

I've mentioned just a few of many family members. However, there were so many biological family members that just blended right in with the church family. These cousins were very close to me because I was in their company more than many others. As I fore stated, Cousin Nina was my baby-sitter as my parents went to work. I would play with her children, as they were my siblings that I had left. I would pretend to be their baby-sitter. Cousin Nina's most memorable moments of me as a child are in church pretending to shout and imitate the church members falling out under the anointing.

CHAPTER FOUR

THE MOLDING BEGAN

Between the ages of four and five the first thing to be put in order was my name. I have now been with my new family for about a year or two. While playing with my dolls, as I often did, I held a conversation with them. I pretended one of the dolls was my mother and I began to talk to her, and got this bursting idea. I ran in and told my Aunt Maggie whom I was now calling Mom. "I must to do something about my name." I told her I was going to freeze the Hunt name. I would no longer be called Carrie Hunt; I was now Carrie Brantley. This brought a smile to my mother's face that I had never seen before. This now gave me a sense of belonging.

Church was now my little life. I was getting ready to go to preschool. I was very small for my age because I was so short. Mother would have me dressed like a little doll with the little "ruffled" dresses with the slip that spreads out the tail of the dress. My hair was in candy curls with ribbons, and I wore the best apparel money could buy. Now my life appears to have taken a turn. Gifts and talents began to come into focus. People began to marvel at a four year old standing on stage, able to recite long stanzas of poetry and speak with authority. I remember during an usher's anniversary at the age of four I recited a poem so well, the people began to stand on their feet applauding the performance. The minister picked me up, put his hand in his pocket, pulled out a dollar (lot of money), and gave it to me. He was so proud of me. I left the stage smiling from ear to ear waving my dollar and my mother beckoned me to her for fear of what my next movement would be. She was elated and gave me the biggest hug and praised me for my accomplishment. I left there feeling very proud. The excitement of my new life began to overshadow the memories of my past.

I became very active and attended Sunday school regularly. I was placed in private nursery school. I began to not only look like the princess I felt like the day I arrived in Florida, but now I felt like I was floating on a cloud. I began private piano lessons and learned very quickly. If there was anything money could buy, Mom got it. However, there was one thing lacking, LOVE.

These were years of my many dreams and joyful times being fulfilled. I can remember sitting alone daydreaming of my family back in Georgia. Sometimes I would be in tears often wondering what made my parents give me away-too young to remember that only my dad gave me away. So I began the search for answers, never asking anyone, but always pondering in my mind, wondering what I could have possibly done to be the child selected from the five to be taken away from the home. I was determined to find the answer to my question, "Why Me?"

At age five, I started private school, excelling in any and everything put before me. I appeared to be a happy child at all times. To this day I know that it was only God that had his hand on my life from the very beginning. I can remember that my tearful times were my personal moments. I thought they were moments that no one heard, later I found out that someone was hearing my cry.

As a child being very inquisitive and very observant I would imitate everything I would see. If I saw you doing it I would try to mimic it exactly. I would stand quietly and just stare, all the while rehearsing the movements in my mind, only to duplicate it when I was alone. I can remember two different incidents that are very vivid in my mind. My mother hired a carpenter to build her some brand new cabinets. He covered the doors and counter tops with a vinyl covering. I stood there watching him trim the counter tops and doors to perfection.

That's why it was so easy for me duplicate, at least I thought it looked easy. When my mother asked me to stay put and to be good until she returned from taking him home; I was obedient for a brief moment. Then temptation got the best of me. I took a knife and began to emulate what I saw the carpenter do. My tiny hand gripped the handle of the knife I took from the counter after climbing onto a chair; I tried to rehearse in my mind exactly what I had seen. I began to scrape the edge of the door. There wasn't as much vinyl as I saw him use. But I used what I had in my possession. I began to plaster the material onto the already finished door. Then I heard the car's engine enter the driveway. I tried to hurry and put the knife down.

Apparently, I was not as fast as I saw myself rehearse it in my mind. To my surprise I heard the door open and I sat on the floor with the knife and the reconstructed door. My mother walked in, but not with a smile on her face. With a grin, showing my pearly whites I stood speechless. There was no denying or convincing her that I didn't do it. Especially since I was the only person left at home. The damage I did to the cabinet and the lie I tried to tell to cover it did not help the fury of the wrath that I was about to experience. The normal spankings I felt on the hand I would have welcomed. My mother didn't bother to get my dad's belt to spank me this time. I received nothing but flesh to flesh - several slaps to various parts of my body. This was the beginning of the abuse. This brief moment appeared to last longer than the sand that flowed from the hourglass in our living room. All of my glory days now appeared to have vanished.

I left the kitchen and went to my bedroom sore, not only physically, but with whelps from the beating. I was only imitating what I saw. I no longer felt like the little princess, my dreams had turned into a nightmare from which I wanted to speedily awake. When my father returned home and saw me he confronted my mother about this matter. She listened to what he had to say, but that didn't change the fact that I was now wearing the scars. I must have been in deep

36

despair, because I usually lit up with joy when I heard him entering the house. One particular time I didn't hear him come in. He came to my room and told me how much he loved me and expressed his hurt. He tried to comfort and to console me, as I lay across my bed in deep thoughts. I enjoyed every moment of being in his presence. My dad was the world to me. He was the definition of love. It seemed he understood when no one else could or would. Because of his love for me he didn't fail to tell me what I did was wrong. He encouraged me to experiment on something else the next time. However, this incident did not stop my curiosity.

The next encounter of my wandering mind and kinesthetic skills occurred in the bathroom. My mother was decorating the bathroom with new curtains for the window and shower, the whole works. Again I stood and watched until she had completed everything and left the bathroom. I picked up the scissors and began to cut out the floral prints and put on the finishing touches. The edges of the patterns weren't clear cut, but they were to the point of my perfection. Need I say what happened when she made the discovery of her newly decorated laboratory? I had actually cut the shower curtain's flowers and attached them to the wall with water. It did stick, at least for a little while.

My helping hand would always get me in trouble, not to mention my curiosity to create. My mind was always working. There was very little even at the age of five and six that I couldn't think my way out. It was only when I lied that I got myself in deep trouble, so I learned at an early age that lying didn't work for me. After getting into trouble with my experiments, you would think this would stop me from exploring with new bursting ideas, but they didn't. Now I can see why I had to explore and venture into the unknown to quench the thirst of my curiosity.

My mother was a very dominant, but giving person. She basically made the decisions in our home. She made sure anyone in need was not left in the same state when she left his or her presence, if she had it in her power to help. She would visit the sick, clean their houses, wash their clothes, do the ironing, or whatever the need was. She truly exemplified being a helper to those in need. The one thing she had a hard time exemplifying to me was the love I longed for in a mother. Then again maybe she didn't know how to share her inner love. Anything monetary was no problem to her as far as giving. This could be the reason God could entrust her and my dad with it. He knew they would give liberally to those in need.

I can remember a time when my mother and some of the saints went to one of the mother's home to help her. I was just a little girl and my parents usually took me with them if they could or let my cousin care for me. This particular time, my mother took me with her. I was allowed to stay in the yard to play with my dolls. I saw those women washing Mother Cobb's clothes on the scrub board (a metal board with ridges enclosed by wood), ironing, cleaning, dusting, cooking, freshening her bed daily, and even bathing her. This was something I didn't think was important at the time, but I later learned the importance of helping those in need. This experience taught me how it is truly done the way the Bible says it should be done, with a heavenly mind. I may have been just a little girl, but what I saw those women do had an impact on my life. I didn't know

38

it was getting into my spirit. They came bringing food to cook and cleaning items. They left with only the supplies they took to do the cleaning. I later found out that she had a stroke and was not able to do anything for herself.

These were happier times with my mother because we were with the saints, and I didn't have a chance to get a beating around them. They only saw this side of my mother, until they were allowed to live with us for an extended period of time.

Our home was always open to church members, the Bishops, State Mothers, and others coming in to do revivals. Other family members who needed a place to start a new life in Sanford were also welcome. My father would many times give up his bed for more space in order to make our guest more comfortable. Our home appeared to be the place of hospitality.

My dad was very quiet, and allowed my mother to make many decisions pertaining to the family. This is why he very seldom questioned her actions, no matter how he may have felt about them. Many people said when I arrived, and came into his life I was his world. They coined the phrase, "The sun rose on my head and set at my feet", and I felt the same way about him. He was a hard working man and made sure I had the best. My father would travel from place to place seeking work. He would always try to come home that night, but if he could not, we expected to see him the next morning at the latest the weekend. My father was a provider, and we lived very well to be considered poor people. I guess he got tired of traveling trying to find employment. He decided to join some of the other members of the church and become a migrant worker.

There were plenty crops to be harvested in many other parts of Sanford and surrounding areas. However, the work was seasonal. In Florida we would pick oranges and other citrus fruit, also some vegetables in season, mainly cabbage and celery. I traveled to the fields with my dad; he and the workers looked out for me. Mom would be running errands or working elsewhere and he would care for me. They very seldom left me in another's care. As fast as my dad would fill a basket, I would take the oranges out and begin to count them. I'm pretty sure I must have counted the numbers over and over again. I would also lay the fruit in rows and stack them one on top of the other. As I reflect back on it, I was a builder even then. I was always trying to find something to do with my hands. I may not have been in school during that time, but the learning continued. The field became my classroom. After all had been done in Sanford we would load up the truck and go to Georgia. There I would have a chance to see my biological family.

The first stop was Dublin, Georgia. Here we would pick up my family and other workers. They would load up the truck with their personal belongings, and we would travel north. This time was special also because I would get to see my siblings again. We would all travel to Virginia to a small town called Atlantic. Believe it or not, this place was smaller than Sanford. Before our departure, Mom would say, "Carrie, make sure you use It before you get back in the car". The "It" was the outhouse. "We don't want to make any unnecessary stops in route." There was no indoor toilet in the country. We were now on our long journey down the dusty back roads of Georgia. If we had to go, we would have to stop alongside the road. We were still in the south. There were little to no facilities where we were welcome. After everyone was aboard, we would sing songs to make the trip's journey seem shorter.

I was excited to see my family again. My oldest sister, Annie made the journey, but she would not work the field. She would stay at the camp and help with the cooking. She was very quiet, reminding me of my adopted father. My sister Jeanelle would spend a lot of time with me expressing how lucky I was to be able to live a much better life. She loved singing. Fearing what might happen if I told them what this great life really entailed I would keep my thoughts and feeling to myself. Even at such an early age I knew to keep silent. My oldest brother, Lester, Jr. was a hard worker and earned just as much money as my real dad when he worked. Herbert, my youngest brother, always stayed home with my mom (Candy).

Due to the different backgrounds of each family, paydays were sometimes happy and sad. My father would use his money wisely and save it for our future during the off season. But there were some families without Christian standards. They would bet their money away, or use it to purchase alcohol and become drunk. When they returned to the camp, their wives would look for the money, and they would have spent it all or had very little. The domestic problems would be very sorrowful, but the next week it would be work as usual.

The potato crops were just about completely harvested, and it was time to move on to the next campsite. My biological family did not take this trip. I don't think they were prepared due to the change in the weather. It was now late August and more potatoes and vegetables such as tomatoes had to be harvested. The workers were now short handed by losing three valuable workers: Jeanelle, Lester, Jr., and my dad. They had to work three times as fast and hard, but they did it. After New York, I thought that was enough, but as I said before, he was a provider. Our last trip was to Canada. This reminded me of the story of the "Ant and the Grasshopper". Daddy would work as hard as he could while he was able, so when times got hard, and he wasn't able there would be a nest egg to carry us over until the next season.

I passed the time away by playing with my dolls and playing with my imaginary friends. Much of my time was spent in my own little world I had created where I was in charge. My life continued on an uphill climb. I loved church; it had become one of the most important parts of my life. The piano lessons continued, Sunday school, and being actively involved in youth services. I was always active when it pertained to events at the church and school. My piano teacher told my mom that I had no need to continue taking lessons because I played by ear. I was allowed to play the piano at church. People began to marvel at the talent the Lord had blessed me with. I wasn't shy or afraid to speak.

CHAPTER FIVE

EARLY CHILDHOOD

My father continued to travel place to place seeking work. This particular year the crops hadn't produced much. He and my mother traveled to Philadelphia, Pennsylvania. There they found work with a white family. We closed up our home and stayed there during the summer. The lady informed my mother that she could let me stay at the house and play with her daughter while she and my dad went to work in the fields. The little girl and I were the same age. Considering the time and laws of the land, my mother felt comfortable to leave me there. I was happy to be able to play with someone my age. We played many games together and read books. She had her dolls and I had mine. The mother was very nice to me. Whatever she gave her daughter I received an equal share. This action by the lady also left an impression on my heart. All people of the other race didn't act the same. She appeared to be very caring.

We found a church in Philadelphia as well. They had service in the same manner as we did back home. They greeted one another with a holy kiss and showed such kindness towards one another. Their church was a little larger than ours was, but the atmosphere was filled with love. When the work was finished we traveled back to Florida just in time for school.

Since the crops weren't as fruitful, I was now enrolled in public school. I was ahead of my grade. I entered public school at age seven, and in the third grade. I was very short and looked as if I were in first grade. My mom made sure I wore the best and made sure I was always neat and clean. My hair was always in place, with ribbons neatly done. This caused some problems for me. I was picked at because I was so little and many of the children didn't like what I wore. The teachers would call on me to answer many questions and I'd run most errands that needed to be done. So you know I was called, "The Teacher's Pet". They would take my lunch money or lunch and dare me to tell my mother. I remember this one day the bigger girls trapped me in the bathroom and challenged me to give them my lunch money. They said if I didn't they were going to put my head down the toilet stool. I was frightened and went home and told my mom. Of course you know my mom confronted their mom. Need I conclude this story? The next day they got me good. I dared not tell her what had happened. I thought if

I told her she may have spanked me and I had already received the torture from my peers. I had just as much fear in me of them as I did my mother at this time. I just felt like an outcast, or misfit. I didn't know where I belonged.

Most memorable moments were spent after school as I walked to my Cousin Nina's house. She was bearing children. She had just had a son. I would pretend to be his baby-sitter as my cousin was mine. The home was filled with love and the family structure was one I looked at to pattern my life after. They set the pace for my spiritual life. The family structure was one I envied. I saw her caress her children and show forth love and they gave it back. I admired the relationship she and her husband had. I saw their love exhibited in the church and home.

I was now about 10 years old, and it was time to travel up north again. I began to prepare my mind to see my friend Daisy. I looked forward to the trips to Virginia. This particular year was different. My mother had something else in mind. She discussed with my dad that I was getting in the way a little too much during harvest time. He agreed reluctantly. Arrangements were made for me to stay with my biological parents. I thought this was great. This is the first time I was allowed to stay such a long period with my real family. I thought it would be fun. I now would be able to spend time with my youngest brother and maybe recapture some of the moments we had missed during our separation.

We packed our bags as usual. My mother began to put almost all of my clothes in the suitcase. I thought this was not normal. My church clothes were packed as well. My mother knew that my biological mom didn't go to church. We continued packing. I dare not ask a question as to why she was doing this. Every pair of shoes I owned went into the luggage. Not thinking anything about it, I loaded my belongings into the car. Mother and I got in the car. My father drove the truck to pick up my dad, Lester, Jr., and Jeanelle. They were going to travel with the rest of the crew. The only sad part about their working was that they were not allowed to go to school.

After I got to the house, I unpacked my bags and greeted my family. We lived in the same city, but I didn't see them everyday although Sanford was a small town. I waved good-bye to my family and went inside with my oldest sister and brother Herbert. My sister had a summer job working for the owners of the corner store. She would clean their house and iron their clothes, and whatever was asked of her. My brother and I had the freedom to roam the streets as we pleased. Mother Candy had gone to do domestic work and at times perform nursing duties in Sanford and other surrounding areas.

I didn't know many of the people in the neighborhood, but many of them knew me. Remember it was church, school, and home for me. I do recall a few faces from school, but I was never allowed to play with them. But this year would be very different. I had freedom–oh freedom! As soon as my brother and I ate breakfast, we were out the door. Many times we would forget the breakfast and would go to visit neighbors and play games and share in their family time. We would stay out until dark. Our sister would keep an eye on us as much as she could. I would hear some of the members of the church say remarks such as, "Look at Carrie out here after dark. She knows her mother would not allow her to do that." Regardless to what they thought, I was living the life I thought was most fun. We had no restrictions, rules, guidelines to follow, or anybody to chastise me as much as I received at home. I'd be out so late that my friends' parents would have a place setting for me at their table. It became an automatic thing. I was no longer a guest, but a part of the family.

My brother and I did not get in much trouble. When we got bored at one friend's house, we would find another one. We would play games such as marbles, jack stones, and we would literally use stones. We would throw the ball up and try to pick up as many stones as we could and catch the ball at the same time. This game would be played on the porch. We would also play "Mother May I". This game was very familiar to me. Those were words that were constantly in my vocabulary. "Hide and Seek" was one of our favorites. This game was played best in the dark. I would always find one of the best places to hide because I was so small. I could hide in some of smallest places you could not imagine. These were some of the happiest times I can remember. I once again could be a child and not have any restrictions placed upon me. I thought this was the life.

This particular summer ended faster than usual. It seemed as though time flew right on by. It was now time for my adoptive parents to come home from their travels. This time my mother was in Georgia sharing the wealth of the increase with family and church members less fortunate. This gave me a chance to talk with my real mom and explain a little of what I was going through. She listened, but told me I was in the best place. She explained that I didn't have to want for anything, and they could give me what she and my dad couldn't. I felt rejected; this again confirmed the fact that no one loved me, except my "Daddy Will". I was afraid of my real dad because his voice was so deep and he appeared to speak so harshly, even when he was greeting someone. I was petrified of my adoptive mother. Now my real mom had let me down, and all I had left was my dad. Here again this was a disappointment to me. I was now ready to see my adoptive Dad. I knew that if anyone loved and understood me, it was he. I wanted to stay with my adoptive parents, but I felt I had no love from my mom. I began to weigh the balance of the two. Do I go where I can be loved, at the same time, whipped and punished for every little thing I do? Or do I stay in this environment with freedom to no end, lack of luxury, and being misunderstood? I may have had an answer, but I was too afraid to voice it to anyone.

Little did I know as these thoughts were going through my mind, my mother had thoughts of her own. I later found out that summer she wanted me to stay with my biological family permanently. I had apparently outgrown that cute little girl she picked up several years ago. No longer able to dress as the little doll, with candy curls anymore, I was now able to make decisions of my own. At times I was a little hard headed, but what child isn't?

The plan was spoiled by the stop she made in Georgia. My dad arrived to pick me up instead of my mother. I was elated to see him. On the way home he asked how my stay was. I told him I really enjoyed it. We arrived home and caught up on one another's summer. Then my mother entered the house. WOW! The look on her face! She was in total shock to see me home. This was one particular time I think my dad would have stood up for me no matter how much she rejected his idea. He truly loved me. I don't know if she resented the fact that Dad and I were so close and shared love without having to give money or anything tangible. We only shared what was from the heart. This she had great trouble doing. From that point, I think the abuse had now risen to its highest level.

For fear of my mother, I tried to do everything right. At this time I had been trained to do most of the house cleaning, cooking, washing dishes, clothes and do the ironing. The clothes were put into a big pot and a fire was lit to get the water hot enough to clean the clothes. There was no hot running water from the faucet. We also made our Argo starch; the clothes had to be ironed to perfection. I remember having to iron the sheets for the bed, my dad's underwear, and shirts. There could not be one wrinkle, or I must do it again. This taught me to give my best and nothing less. God strives for perfection (He wants our best). During those days the irons were placed on the wood burning stove and when one was hot, I ironed with that one, exchanged the other and continued to rotate. I cleaned the floors on my hands and knees. Mother always wanted the house to be nice and clean. She trained me to do this work and made sure it was done correctly. I began to think I was adopted just to become her housekeeper.

I also learned to cook many meals at an early age. I was glad when I finally could cook for my dad. There were many times when he had to cook for me. My mother would buy grocery and dare my dad and me to touch it. If we had company, they were welcome to eat it. However, we were not allowed to touch it unless we were cooking it for her. It appeared we were two separate families living under one roof. It seemed as though we had become so divided. My dad would do the shopping for us and buy little snacks for me so I wouldn't have to ask her for them.

I can recall entering the seventh grade and my mother forbidding me to go on this particular field trip. I really wanted to attend. I can't recall why she forbade me to go. When I received the permission form I signed it, and saved enough of my allowance to pay for the trip. My mother paid one of the seniors to pick me up for school and carry me home. I had the trip all planned, but my plan had one flaw in it. I failed to look on the form to see what time we were to return to school after the field trip, I assumed it was like all the others. As the roll was called for us to line up, and the teacher examined the parent signatures I sat anxiously awaiting my name. I was instructed to line up. Therefore, I passed the first part of this test. I proceeded in line, and I got on the bus. We arrived, and I was so excited because you know it is usually church, school, home, and the circle continued. The field trip was great! It was now time for lunch. We had eaten lunch, and the time was approaching dismissal from school. However, the teacher announced the second half of the field trip. I began to panic and asked, "When are we leaving?" I was made aware that the form said we will arrive back an hour later. I tried to relax through the second half of the trip. I now decided, "Hey, why not enjoy it. I'm already in trouble."

But the trip home felt like traveling from Sanford to Dublin. I sat picturing my mother's fury in my mind when she found out I had disobeyed her. The picture did not look pretty at all. I finally arrived at my destination. My mother was spotted at a neighbor's house. She had been informed that I wasn't on the bus, but had been detained due to the field trip. She proceeded with her conversation. I walked toward the house and went to my room. Thoughts raced through my head. "What will this woman's next move be?"

Now, Ma Dear, as I called her, entered the door. She was not enraged, but strikingly peaceful. Now I *really* did not know where the missing piece was to the puzzle. She walked in and asked how was my day with a serene tone of voice, which was very rare at a time like this. I responded. She said, **"I told you not to go to the field trip, didn't I?"** My response was, **"Yes ma'am"**. She then asked why did I do it. I answered the most commonly used word in a child's vocabulary, **"I don't know"**. She said nothing else.

To my surprise, we ate dinner; I cleaned the kitchen, got my bath, and prepared for bed. I tossed and turned at first not knowing what my punishment would be. Then I finally went to sleep. But oh, the next morning I woke up to an extension cord coiled around my mother's hand. She folded it in half. It was doubled its power. I felt a draft on my body. Not awake just yet, I tried to pull the covers back over me just to have them snatched completely off my body. The cord she beat me with was a detachable iron cord. I lay helpless in my bed. She beat me so much, I blistered and whelped until my skin began to separate showing the impression of each lash I received. The blood was oozing from my wounds. The sight of blood didn't stop her. The force behind the whipping was filled with what appeared to be a reaction of so much hatred I would wish upon no one. I recall screaming to her how sorry I was and promising it will never happen again. The beating continued. I received lashes across my back, arms, legs, hands, anywhere the cord connected, I felt its sting. She had gotten her satisfaction and immediately told me to get ready for school. I searched my closet in the midst of my tears for a long sleeved blouse to cover my wounds.

I went to the bathroom and prepared myself for school. Upon dressing, I left the house carrying my books erect in my hands to refrain from them touching my branded skin. I can almost relate to the cattle getting branded. I don't think their pain was as severe. As I reached the school, my eyes were blood shot. I tried to hold back the sniffles from my peers, but the agony was superseding my power to endure. I made it to the room only to have all eyes on me. The students, in such a thoughtful caring way, expressed their feelings to the teacher. The teacher called me to her desk to relieve me of so much attention. She began to immediately tend to my wounds. I just wanted someone to hold me and show me he really loved me. My teacher inquired. I explained, but her hands were tied due to no child abuse laws during this era. The motto was, "Spare the rod spoil the child". This one scripture my mother practiced wholeheartedly. I tried to concentrate the whole day, but could only stare into space. The teacher understood and let me stay in my own little world. I could tell her heart went out to me. Only prayer could change this situation, and deep down inside, I believe she did just that, pray. My teachers were very sweet and many were God fearing women.

When I arrived home, my daddy was sitting in the living room reading. He noticed my bruises and for the first time, I heard him elevate his voice and stand up to my mother. After hearing his complaint, she shut her door and locked the deadbolt lock on it and told him the couch was his bed for the night. So we sat on the couch consoling one another. We were alone on our little island, just my father and me. I would love to say the abuse ended here, but it didn't. Somehow God gave me the strength to weather the storm.

God taught me a lesson of obedience through my beatings. I often wondered how a person so thoughtful and generous to others could be so cruel to beat a child so mercilessly. My 7th grade year was a trying time for me. I knew that there was no way a person could endure such a thing without God on his side. I wasn't even saved and knew this much. To add to that traumatic experience, I had to be retained. I had missed too many days of school. There was hope in the midst of this confused situation. My teacher had a conference with my mom and explained to her that I could attend summer school and be promoted. My mother told her to go ahead and retain me and not look forward to my attending summer school. This was the time we were to travel to Virginia. My parents didn't want to leave me with anyone again. They didn't want me to get adjusted to a life without discipline or structure.

I could only think about graduation. I would not graduate with my class, and wondered what they would have to say about me now. They already talked about me, now they have one more piece of information to put on their agenda. I thought she was trying to hurt me again, but deep down inside I felt like she was making the right decision. I may not have told my adoptive parents this, but I did want supervision and discipline, just not so severe. She tried to make me feel better reiterating the fact that I was a year ahead of my class, and now I am right where I belong. My size was also taken into consideration. I handled it. I didn't like it, but there was nothing I could do about it.

CHAPTER SIX

THE MIGRANT LIFE

It is time to travel again. Things will be a little different this year. Daddy is now the "Crew Leader". Daddy saw how lucrative the business was and the opportunity came to him, and he accepted it. He had been scouting out various areas and had now decided to take on the responsibility. Some of the responsibilities included making sure the workers arrived at each destination safely and appropriating the crew workers' just pay. Those who were members of his team were privileged. Many crew leaders were not as loyal as my dad was. He also made sure we had the best sleeping arrangements. If it was not good enough for him, it was not good enough for his crew.

55

Quite a few of the crew workers were members of the family and church. There were some that didn't belong to either. However, they came along with the same goal in mind. This was to provide for their families and try to save enough to help during the off season or in times of drought. Soon my biological father's life was fully committed to the Lord. The booze was longer in the picture. He became an ordained minister. If we traveled to a place without a church, we had all we needed to have our own services, which we did so often. If it was just prayer and worship service, we acknowledged God and was ever grateful for his blessings.

Our journey began in Florida with the citrus. The next stop was Dublin, Georgia. Now that my family was living in Sanford, the excitement wasn't as great as once before. Although we weren't getting my family, others remained and needed to be picked up. I no longer traveled with the dolls I thought that was not appropriate for a girl my age. I was approaching that age that parents dread, the teen years where one thinks he knows more than his parents do, yet needs them to provide those clothes he wants to wear, and can't afford.

It is now 1952 and the south is not such a peaceful place right now. The Florida secretary of the NAACP, Harry T. Moore and his wife were just killed as someone bombed their home on Christmas night this past year. Racial tension was still high. We had to be very careful how and where we drove. We traveled HWY 17, and did our best not to break any laws. We would sing songs to take our mind off the problems that existed in the south. This seemed to shorten the travel time also. I couldn't wait to see my friend Daisy, in Atlantic, VA. We befriended one another a few years earlier.

As we traveled and daylight came I would watch the scenery from our '46 Chevy. I had now advanced to the front seat of the car. When I was younger I knew that my permanent seat was in the back. This particular year my mother allowed me to sit in the front. I think it was done to help ease the pain of my recent failure. I enjoyed the times when we could act like mother and daughter, not predator and prey. I would look forward to the ride on the ferryboat to get across to the Chesapeake Bay. There are some things we never outgrow.

Here in Virginia we would unload the trucks. There would sometimes be anywhere from fifteen to twenty people on one truck. Then a law passed prohibiting too many workers on one truck. My dad had two trucks one for the supplies, and the other for the people. The main crops were potatoes, but other vegetables were also plentiful. It was in this place where I have many fond memories of church, also.

There was no piano player, and only a small youth choir. I got an abundance of training here in this little town that remains even today. I loved working with the children; it made me feel like a little leader. At the time I wasn't aware that I was in training to become a leader. I just enjoyed working and helping in the church. I directed the choir, led songs, and played the piano.

Daisy was older than I, but she made me feel very special and gave me a ray of hope stressing the fact that I was important and had a lot of good to offer many people. She could have found friendship in my older sisters since they were more her age, however, she chose to be my friend until this day. She and I would play games, sing, and soon after share stories with one another. These moments would last long enough for me to have something to look forward to 'til next year.

This particular year Daisy, and I, and several other children decided to go and pick some berries after our work was done. We had a ball throwing berries at each other and eating them after wiping them on our clothes. After playing in the fields, I returned to the campsite running like all the other children, only to hear my mother scold me. She began to hit me right there on the field. I now had some witnesses to see what goes on behind closed doors. This time it wasn't my "Daddy Will" that stood up to her, it was my biological father. After this beating, I can't recall getting another. I finally felt like someone was more powerful than my mom was. She says she told me not to go pick berries. I told her I honestly didn't hear her make this statement.

After we left Virginia in August we headed for New York. We remained until November. The crops in New York were potatoes and other veggies such as string beans and tomatoes; there were also apples. I was now at an age where I helped cook for the crew and did other odd jobs I was able to perform. The leaves this time of the year were a pretty red and gold. I have always been attracted to the beauty of nature. This was the year my sister Annie came along on the journey. After we made it to New York she decided she would stay up north with my mother's sister, Aunt Carrie. There were generations of Carries'. I was the Carrie for my generation. I guess migrant work wasn't the lifestyle for her. She made a life for herself in Detroit, Michigan. She could no longer endure the pressures of the south.

My father was an honest man and people trusted him; he was a man of integrity. He and mom would bring extra supplies for the people to put on credit until they received their pay. I can remember there was good money to be made. One year as a little girl I was allowed to ride with Daddy, and he allowed me to count the money he had earned. I think I counted over three hundred dollars. It was so much money to me. As I can recall this is when we started saving money to buy the trucks. We were prepared for this moment. Daddy was a smart man. He was not only looking out for my mom and me. He never forgot those in the church or the family. He provided those in need with fruits and vegetables. Another man made sure that everyone had fish and other seafood. If we were all together, we remained just that, together.

During this time God was placing things in my spirit I wasn't aware of such as unity. I may not have experienced it at home, but when we traveled I had such a large family and felt protected by all. I know it was God who kept me from all hidden dangers of the world. There were many dangers facing us as we traveled. I was in the presence of some children that had been raped, or had children out of wedlock. There were many things happening in the fields that only God could have protected me from. I was privileged to have been in a Christian environment. I didn't think so then, but as I look at it today I am truly blessed.

There were men who drank and had no respect for women, children, or themselves. At times they would curse their wives, then go drink, spend all their money, come back, and want to beat their wives. My father had to intervene many days. Not only did they fight their wives, they fought other men as well over gambling and playing cards. This is why I say I am appreciative for my training. I was exposed to the life, but never desired to engage in its lifestyle. I could have been like some of these people, but I thank God for my parents instilling religious values in me. During these times, men did feel inferior not being able to be called a man, but boy. This could drive some to the bottle or other outlets. I'm glad my dad turned to Jesus. Through their prayers, others that drank, smoked, cursed, gambled, and other habits in which they were held captive, were delivered. My biological father was a living example of that.

My father didn't isolate himself with only church people. He would be in the midst of those in need of a solution to their problem. Many thought the problem was money and not enough of it for their behaviors. The saints were there to encourage them differently. All didn't have to attend church services with us, but many times we were so loud there was no choice but to join in with us. Then there were no other outlets, except church or the bottle. Many chose the bottle over the church. The bottle relieved their sorrows for a moment and set them back even farther, but this wasn't realized until they were exposed to the real truth. Being in the midst of our family, and my father being in that authoritative position, helped bring many families to Christ. My mother was a true Christian in bringing in the souls, even in the fields. She just had such a hard time showing her love to those closest to her. Many souls were won to Christ through their lives. Out on the fields they did work together as a team.

This is one reason I love to travel seeking those who are lost. As I reflect, this was true training ground. Literally working the natural fields bringing in the harvest, but God had placed in my spirit that we were harvesting natural fruits and vegetables before they died. He also sees to it that the souls of men need to be harvested before they die. My experiences on the field as a child would never be forgotten because each fruit or vegetable picked represented a soul. Langston Hughes wrote it perfectly:

MY PEOPLE

The night is beautiful,
And so the faces of my people,
The stars are beautiful,
So the eyes of my people.
Beautiful, also, is the sun.
Beautiful, also, are the souls of my
People.

LANGSTON HUGHES

CHAPTER SEVEN

TEEN YEARS

I lived the life of a normal teenager. I went to school and was involved in many activities during the day. I went through the rebellious stage. I tried to live a double life one for church, and another for school. I tried to hang with the "In Crowd". Although I did all these things, my life was very sheltered. I felt like a bird in a cage waiting for the door to come open just to spread my wings. I must be compatible to a carrier pigeon (one trained to carry messages); I'd fly at school, but report right back home for the next task. Life at home got better. Mom and I even had pleasant moments as we went grocery shopping. One particular incident happened in the car when we were talking, I guess I got a little too playful. We were unloading the car of the grocery. I began to laugh at something she said. I thought nothing of it; I was glad we could laugh together. I was walking in the house with a bag of grocery in my arms and felt this brush of wind pass my face. I heard a bang! It was the canned good landing on the floor. My mother had thrown it at me because I was laughing. I thought I was laughing with her but maybe she thought I was laughing at her.

Despite her ways, I had a good life as a teen. I just had to watch my steps carefully. My chores were done without having to be told. I was trained to do them very early. They were performed, as one would remember to brush his teeth on a daily basis. Before doing anything on the weekend I had to make sure the house was spotless. Therefore, on Fridays I would come home from school and do everything. The bathroom was cleaned, the floor mopped, dusting was done, and I would even get an early start on the laundry. We now owned a wringer washing machine. Mother made sure she kept up to date with the latest appliances to make MY job easy. She would come home to find everything spick and span. Saturday morning I wanted to sleep late. My mother would wake me to clean the house. I dare not say anything. I would get up and move about until she had to go somewhere. I'd get back in the bed and rest until I heard the car's engine. I would wash the baseboards weekly, and clean the windows. There was no such thing as spring-cleaning; it was done on a more regular basis. This may have sounded harsh, but this too trained me to become a person meticulously clean and neat.

On weekends when not allowed to go anywhere, I'd sit and watch the television or read the newspapers or magazines. The big thing in the news during this time was Brown v. Board of Education. "The law is passed; schools are to integrate." The white schools now had to accept black students and black schools the same to whites. The news headline read "HIGH COURT BANS SCHOOL SEG-REGATION; 9 - 0 DECISION GRANTS TIME TO COMPLY." Each state had a certain time to fulfill the law. This was 1954 I was a freshman in high school. I graduated in a class of only black students.

My teen years were my "Hey Days", I was allowed to participate in many activities. I guess we as teens had the attitude of, "respect me I'm almost an adult". But deep down inside we longed to continue to be children. These years were glory years, but also years of trying to find out who I really was. I tried not to succumb to peer pressure. If you really come to grips with yourself, it is hard trying to do it on your own. I remember dressing one way at home and when I reached a friend's house I changed into something else. I started out wearing a dress, but by the time I got to school I was wearing pants and maybe a little lipstick. I had a figure that I thought looked better in pants. I could show the curves that were hidden under this skirt. I was not allowed to wear lipstick or pants at home. Our church doctrine stated these stipulations in the rules. During my early teen years, I didn't have a desire to go to church as I did when younger. After all I thought I could do some things, I had not professed salvation.

While in high school I was very popular. I was involved in clubs like; Future Homemakers of America (FHA), Student Council,

Drama Club, Future Nurses Club of America, I was a Cheerleader and voted Junior Class Sweetheart. I had one of the leading roles in our Senior Class play. I loved going to school; this was where I was free to be me. I wasn't loose, but I enjoyed being a teenager. I was approaching the age that I set goals for college. My intent was to attend a college far from home. My mother was saving money for me to attend. This would be an honor. Many blacks were just being allowed to attend many prestigious colleges.

Mother may have treated me differently, but she did love me. She had to pray about where I would attend college for riots were breaking out in many southern colleges and universities. Society was having great difficulty. A student was expelled in Alabama because of her color, although the law said she was eligible to attend. Racial differences dictated she can't. Blacks now have opportunities to attend any college they are qualified.

I didn't have many girlfriends. I did have quite a few male friends. I enjoyed holding conversation with them. As a matter of fact, one of the members of the church was a very close friend during high school. He loved to draw. We called him "Skeet". His name was really Robert. Because I associated with more males than females, I was labeled as being fast. My mother continued to buy me nice clothes. I didn't change outfits everyday on the way to school. I did it sporadically. Many girls were jealous of my relationships with the guys, and my parents' ability to buy me nice apparel. After all I wasn't allowed to wear jewelry but, I could at least wear the latest fashions within reason. I tried the jewelry bit also. I was also allowed to drive to school my senior year. Both my parents had cars.

By now my mom and I had developed a pretty good relationship.

The teachers showed great love for me, and I loved my teachers. Again I was called upon to do many things. Having to repeat the seventh grade was not as bad as I thought it would be. I was with peers of my own age. I was still smaller than most, but I fit right in with the rest of the group.

Church was an interesting part of my life. I tried to steer away from it, but I found myself being compelled even stronger the next time. I was playing the organ at church for the choir and continued to help with the youth department. My cousin, Nina, now had a much larger family; the children were old enough to play games and understand the rules. I would have them listening to what I told them to do and watch them play church. In addition, we would play different board games to pass the time. Their father was a preacher. We sang at various churches prior to his preaching. We had our own singing group. Those were the days!

On Easter Sunday morning in 1957, as I sat in church with my sister-in-law I told her I was going to get saved. She responded, "Yeah, right!" I tried convincing her of how serious I was concerning this matter. She didn't believe me. In a way I needed a little convincing myself. I knew within my heart that this is what I wanted to do. But somehow I couldn't find my way to the altar. I remained on my seat.

CHAPTER EIGHT

REAL LOVE-MEETING JESUS

While I was in school during my junior year, a strange feeling came over me. The Lord was really dealing with my heart, and I couldn't shake this from my mind. My mind was turning with different things. I couldn't wait to get home fast enough. I thought that maybe the feeling would subside. I had never felt this way. The closer I got to my house, the feeling got stronger. It felt like something was tugging at my heart. I was sixteen years old. This was my third year at Crooms High School. When I reached my home and saw my mom and dad I asked them if they were going to attend church service on tonight. This was strange. I was usually the one not wanting to go to church. I knew the only young people to be in attendance was the Pastor's son and myself. They said they were not going. As soon as I heard they weren't going, I called my Cousin, Nina. I asked if she was going to service. She said she and her family were going to attend. I asked if she could pick me up and she did.

At church, I sat much closer to the front than usual. I felt an urgency to make it to the altar to pray. The minister was having praise and worship service. This particular night was prayer meeting. The routine was to have the scripture and a song. However, this short devotion appeared too long. After the scripture was read, he sang an old hymn. I had great expectations on this night. I will never forget this night as long as I live and have breath in my body. Once the hymn was finished, all desiring prayer were welcomed to come to offer God their sacrifice. This night will be the greatest sacrifice of all. The church wasn't packed, but I knew I had to make it to the altar even if there were a crowd. I had determined in my mind that tonight would be my night.

I made it to the altar with nothing and nobody on my mind but Jesus. I felt in my spirit that I was meeting someone special. I made up in my mind I had been in church long enough without having my personal experience. The time was out for hearing everyone's testimony of how good God is. I wanted to have my very own experience. I can't quite remember making it to the altar. Jesus met me half way with His arms stretched forth just for me. The only memory I have of this experience is crying out to God saying, "Save me Lord Jesus, Help Me". My expectations were not high enough for what took place in my life. I remember very little about what was happening around me.

All I felt was this warm feeling in my body, and a love that erased everything not like God. When Jesus came into my life I was in awe. Words cannot express the feeling I felt that night. This is a moment I will never forget; it was a night of rejoicing. I cannot express what went on. I know I felt free, no pain, all the misery of my past was now given to my savior. I found joy and a peace I thought was impossible. I didn't want to lose what I had found. I didn't look the same. When the writer wrote, "Your hands looked new," it was a reality. I just wasn't the same. Everything appeared new. I had a new prospective or outlook on life. All the misery and years of abuse I had experienced was now forgotten. This love did not compare.

When the Lord got through with me I found myself underneath a pew. Maybe this was the reason people called holiness church-goers "Holy Rollers". That night you could have called me what you desired to call me it wouldn't have mattered to me. I was so weak. I could not even walk, I believe this was the cleansing process. I just couldn't remain the same. Before leaving the altar I made a covenant with God, "Never let me return to where I came". After they helped me up, they carried me to the car and took me home.

Upon my arrival Mother met us at the door. She was so happy for me. My cousin began to tell her what happened at church. My mother had a sparkle in her eyes I'd never seen before. They carried me to bed. All I could do was thank God for my new life. I found my true love. He was everything to me. I could take Him with me every-where. This love far exceeded the love received from my father.

It seems today that salvation is like a microwave; things are done so quickly. I'm so glad it wasn't invented during my time of salvation. I just couldn't go back into the same things from which the Lord saved me. My time at the altar allowed the Lord to perform all the cleansing processes needed for my future. But today, people come to the altar, they shed a few tears and think that is it. My God has not changed. He's too precious to me. Today they have made God too sophisticated. I had no control of what God was doing in me. I'm sure mucous was dripping from my nostrils, I drooled, screamed to the top of my voice, my hair was no longer in tact, my dress may have risen a little maybe even a lot, but it did not matter to me. Apparently I rolled on the floor, but I didn't care. I met my lover. I did what it took to please Him. Think about your first love. Whatever it took to please that person you did it because you loved him. It didn't matter if family and friends saw something different you only saw one thing (LOVE). This is the best description I can compare it with.

I felt like my past was left behind me. I could attest to what Paul said in Philippians 3:13-14. "Brethren, I count not myself to have apprehended: but this one thing I do, forgetting those thing behind, and reaching forth unto those things which are before, I press toward the mark for the prize of the high calling of God in Christ Jesus." I just wanted to press to perfection. I told Him I didn't want to go back and I asked him to keep me. Through finding Him I found peace, love, joy, happiness, I'd never felt before. I didn't want to do anything contrary to what the preacher said would displease Him.

When I woke up the next morning my mother knew I was in no condition to go to school. She called my real mother and asked if she would sit with me until she came back from work. This particular day, 43 years ago 1955, I could do nothing but bask in His glory. My mother didn't disturb me. I think this was an experience for her.

The next day I did go to school. The whole campus looked different. All the students knew there was a change in me. My countenance was different; there was a glow. It reminded me of the stories I read about Moses, and when he spent time with God. I now had a similar experience. When in the presence of God, you can't remain the same. My whole outlook on life was seen with new light. The search was over. I had some of the missing pieces to the puzzle being placed in their proper location. My purpose for living is now being fulfilled. My times of daydreaming, looking up in the sky at the stars at night, and many unanswered questions are now coming into focus. Here is my ray of hope. I now have Jesus I'm no longer alone. I was searching for a savior. In Him I found that and more.

It all took place in my mind. My life now had some direction. I allowed Him to take control and I would never let go of his hand. This is the beginning of purpose in my life and He can direct my path. I had Jesus and that was enough. I had new hope, new meaning and He was real to me. I had someone to talk to at night. In fact He was so real to me I would pull up a chair beside me and talk. I know this sounds crazy, especially for a teenager. My chair had now replaced the dolls I talked to so often when I was younger.

This experience seems as if it happened on yesterday. He rescued me from the bondage of sin, my mind, and life in general. I don't know what I could have become had He not saved me when He did. He did a complete work all in one day. I received Salvation and His precious Holy Ghost right there at the altar. Then I knew that I would be kept. There is no need to back up anymore. He has promised to be everything to me (Mother for the motherless, Father for the fatherless). I adore Him. Having Him direct my path I couldn't go wrong. I had so much joy it didn't seem real.

People talked about me, but that didn't matter. For the first time in my life I was HAPPY from the inside out. My joy was challenged, but He let me know he was in control and directing my life.

He was dealing with my spirit. He would instruct me to do things I wasn't sure of, but I'd do whatever He said. I found peace, as I walked near the river. We lived in downtown Sanford, just a few blocks away from the river. It is the St. Johns River, the only river that flows in the opposite direction of all other rivers. I'd walk along the waterfront and watch the sun's reflection, as it would set on the still waters late in the evenings. It was a beautiful sight. No matter how many times I'd see this same sun and river, it never looked the same. Each time there was something new and different about it. It was as if God gave new meaning to each new sunset. Little did I know that I was communing with God as I was in deep meditation just staring out into the open skies? I marveled at His creation. I'd think in my mind of how awesome He was to have nothing at all everything void and make such beautiful spatial objects. Then He decided to think of me and make me special. I felt special because He chose a little nothing and nobody like me to share his love. I loved to pray to Him and have that assurance that He heard every prayer uttered. He was so real to me I would pull up a chair, close my eyes, and talk with the Lord. I knew that he wasn't there physically and there was nothing wrong with me. This is how real He had become to me. I thought nothing was wrong with my talking with my dolls, and I knew they weren't going to respond back. In prayer I would thank Him so often and tell Him that I would do nothing to hurt or disappoint Him. My mind was my source of communication with my savior. I would use my mind to illustrate how I wanted to live, act; how I wanted my future, my behavior, all these things, I outlined in my mind. I didn't know to reach God, it began in the mind. I reflected on the scripture in Philippians 2:5, "Let this mind be in you, which was also in Christ Jesus:" All these things were being recorded in my spirit. I later found out that the mind is the spirit.

The Lord would speak to my spirit. I wanted to do whatever He instructed me to do. My first test of obedience was a trip to the post office. He spoke to me and told me to get up and go to the post office. I didn't know why, I just felt an urgency to go. I immediately got up and proceeded, headed in the direction of the post office. As I began to walk, I began to think about my mother having a box there, but I didn't have the key. I continued on my first mission for God. I didn't know what to expect I just knew I had to go. We lived on Seventh Street and the post office was on First Street. I had to walk about 15 blocks. In my mind I'm anticipating with great expectation of something extraordinary going to happen. Different things were running through my mind. I reached my destination and said, "Lord I'm here!" This was said in my mind. I saw nothing new. There were people there so I walked over to my mother's box and looked as if I was checking it for mail. Although nothing miraculous happened I felt good about going. I felt a peace because I did what He asked me to do. This trip to the post office would lie dormant in my spirit. This test of obedience would have meaning a couple years later.

This was now my senior year in high school. I continued to be active, but some things I just didn't participate in. No one had to tell me that there were some activities I could not or should not become involved with. If I couldn't take Jesus with me I didn't need to go. I would carry my Bible with me everywhere I went; it was a part of my curriculum. It became one of my required textbooks. When I left home dressed appropriately there was no reason to go to a friend to change. I was happy being who I was. I was a light for Jesus and a beacon for my peers. The words, "If I be lifted up I'll draw all men unto me," was a reality to me. Many young people began to hang out with me. As I aforementioned, I gained the trust of my parents to drive to school. I went to school and came home. I was now popular with Jesus.

Graduation time had come. I had no desire to attend the Senior Prom. My girlfriend and I stayed home, but we helped decorate for this occasion. The year was great. I did nothing that would take me contrary to God's plan for my life. I participated in church activities wholeheartedly. I had plans for after graduation. My mother had saved money for college, but I planned to work for at least a year, then enroll into a college. These were my plans. But God had the master plan.

CHAPTER NINE

THE CALL

It is now post graduation. This summer like all other summers we routinely traveled to Atlantic, Virginia to work the fields. When we reached the city I found out that my friend, Daisy had found me a job away from the fields. It was at a chicken factory. The work was in an assembly line. My mom and dad consented to my working there this year and not the fields. I had graduated, but gave my parents the respect they were due. Daisy wanted me to stay in Virginia with her and her family. My parents agreed. She had come to Florida during my junior year of school. She planned to stay, but had to return. She lived with us for about two months before she discovered she was pregnant. She had an adorable little girl.

I had made plans to stay until January. I wanted to save enough money to enroll in college the semester I got back home. We made very good money. We had the privilege of working overtime. I had no responsibilities, so I saved my money. We were both saved now and enjoyed going to church. I played the piano and sang. This is the place where I had planted my roots, and now they began to sprout. Every time we came to Virginia I played the piano and directed the youth choir. We did almost everything together. We even shared the same bed. We were living in her parents' home and had only the one room. She slept to the head, the baby slept in the middle, and I took the foot of the bed. We would work together in the church, travel to Philadelphia and Washington, D.C. together. We enjoyed each other's company.

For some reason, I wasn't satisfied with my service to the Lord. This was November 1957 I was 18 years old. I had another life changing experience. While working in the factory there was a lot of water we had to work in. I tried wrapping up before journeying outdoors, but somehow I developed a sore throat. I had been inquiring of the Lord about doing more for Him. The first step was my singing. I told the Lord I wanted him to increase my singing ability and playing the piano. I was proving faithful with what He had blessed me with, but I couldn't rest this yearning in my spirit to do more for God. I went on a fifteen day fast. I'd eat nothing all day, and at night I'd eat a bowl of soup. One particular night I came home feeling so bad I forfeited the bowl of soup. This night I went directly to bed. The lights were out; we all retired early. I lay down, but couldn't go to sleep. The excruciating pain became almost unbearable. I cried out to the Lord. It was just a simple prayer. I laid my hand on my throat and whispered, "Lord if you heal my throat I'll be so grateful." Instantaneously, my throat stopped hurting. I swallowed and felt no pain. I had never experienced anything like this before. I had always heard people talking about how He moved for them, but this baffled me beyond belief. I believed it because it happened to me, but here again, He blew my mind. Again I proceeded to touch my throat and took another swallow, even bigger this time. No pain! Then the spirit of the Lord made His presence known in that tiny dark filled room. Bursting with excitement, expressing much gratitude I said, "Lord, you healed me; you touched my throat; anything you want me to do I'll do it, I am so grateful." Then all of a sudden a bright light illuminated the room. He spoke to my spirit and said, "PREACH MY GOSPEL!" All my joy went away as quickly as it came. I fell back down on the bed. I tried to do it in a way not to wake the baby or my friend Daisy. I inquired of the Lord again. I said, "Are you sure you have the right one Lord?" We had a serious conversation. I began to reason with Him, "Lord, I don't even read my Bible, as I should, are you SURE?" Just as I repeated the question, He repeated his statement. I eased myself down gracefully in the bed not to arouse anyone. I had my word out and I made a promise to the Lord, that I didn't want to do anything to hurt him and wanted Him to direct my path. I made an agreement with the Lord. "Lord if you want me to preach your gospel then confirm your word by having people tell me and not me tell them." I don't know what made me say this. I just wanted to be sure.

This experience was rehearsed in my mind as I lay on the bed until I dozed off to sleep. I woke up with it on my mind. I was a little frightened. But there was no doubt in my mind that I had heard the voice of the Lord. I believe God placed it in my spirit to not give attention to the words man would say regarding God not calling a woman to preach. Man didn't call me, so there was no fear of the words they would say. I had laid my Bible down after high school. I picked it up again. While on lunch hour I'd read sometimes instead of eat. I had gone on extensive fasts. Fasting had become a part of my life. Reading the word of God had also become a part of my life. One particular day soon after this experience, one of my co-workers that worked next to me began talking to me and said, "You have a call on your life and when you start preaching I want you to come to my church." Thereafter many confirmations came, "You're going to be a preacher, God has a call on your life." Even the minister at the church I was attending began to tell me the same thing. He would say you are going to be a missionary. I didn't tell a soul even after they were making these statements. I didn't say yea or nay. This went on about a month with God confirming His word. The experience occurred after Thanksgiving. It is now around Christmas time. I didn't share this news with anyone, not even my friend and confidante Daisy.

My trip to Virginia left me with another life changing experience. Those few months seemed to last a lifetime (September through December). The Lord began to impress upon my heart to go back home to Florida. I immediately took heed. I packed my bags and told Daisy and her parents I was going back home. I loaded my car and left December of that same year. As soon as I reached Florida family and church members began to notice the change. They knew that God had made a difference in my life, they saw the call in my life.

I will never forget it was a Friday night my parents and I went to church to prayer meeting. I was at the piano and the conductor of the service called for testimonies. December 21, 1957 I stood up and began to testify about my experience in Virginia. I had held this secret between God and me for one complete month without telling anyone. By the time I finished testifying there wasn't a dry eye in the building. For they knew that God had done it. They could see the change God had done in my life. From that moment 'til this I would never be the same again. Things began to happen that only He could do. My calling became more of a reality.

Every New Years' Eve the pastor would call on the missionaries to give a word with a five minute time period to speak. This year the pastor called me to speak. After the news had spread many family members and friends even classmates came to hear this message that would last for five minutes. I diligently prayed and fasted to get a word from God for my first trial sermon.

On December 31st, many of my family members and peers were there at church to hear this message. I approached the podium with my Bible in my hand and the Lord had me to ask the question, "Sinner Man Where You Gonna' Run?" I only asked the question and gave my text; the rest is history. That moment the church went up. Everyone that sat under the sound of my voice knew that God called me.

God put His seal of approval on my calling. If He didn't prove it to anyone else I know without a shadow of a doubt He is a man of His word. God began to open doors. The pastor gave me permission to run my first revival January 1958. The church was packed. God met us there. Two souls gave their lives to the Lord. Calls began to come from everywhere along the East Coast of Florida. I was well known because of the traveling done by my mother while performing missionary work. She was also one of the State Mothers. Young people began to come to the Lord in large numbers.

I was on the road for Jesus. He kept His promise to me and I vowed to keep my vow with him. If there were programs or events and the church needed a speaker they didn't hesitate to call on me. I enjoyed working for Jesus. After all, He was the one who came and rescued me. I owed Him so much He saved my life. I can be a vessel for him to use and a mouth for Him to speak through. I wanted nothing and no one to interfere with the relationship He and I had. I had a friend who would not fail me. I have had a cherished relationship with God for forty-three years of unbroken service, and I will always make myself available to him. At age 16 I gave him my life and made a covenant with Him that he could use me. Then at age 18 He called me because He knew He could trust me to carry His gospel. I will let nothing separate me from His love. He took a little nobody and made something beautiful out of my life; He allowed me to see the purpose for which I was made and who I am. I don't know why He chose me, but I'm so glad he did. I am proud to say I am that little carrier pigeon, "TRAINED TO CARRY MESSAGES," and blessed with the name "Carrie".

CHAPTER TEN

A TRAGIC ENDING

At age 18 my ministry is coming alive. I know God has called me and ordained me to carry His word. I now feel I have a purpose in life. The call has been placed on my life. However, nothing I set out to do was successful. I tried working at various jobs, but none gave me the satisfaction as working for God in His house. I have a job to dedicate my life to; I cherished His word. I felt like I was needed and knew that God loved me. Now it's not only the love of my dad, but now I have Jesus. I always wanted to please these two (my adopted dad and God). God had given me the assurance He called me and He loved me.

I traveled up and down the coast of Florida in my ministry. My second revival after Sanford was in Jacksonville. I would get a little work here and there to support myself. But my life was centered around the word and preaching in revivals telling what thus said the Lord. I had no training. At this time there were no Bible colleges to attend. There were few evangelists and little training in our church, but I had the Holy Ghost, which is a keeper and teacher. If you said you had a calling you were put in the pulpit. This was your training ground.

I thank God for training me. He didn't allow me to go from church to church just to deliver the word to the people, but he also taught me the meaning of many of the gifts He had placed in my life. As I journeyed to Jacksonville I didn't feel alone. Many of the ministers took me under their wing. I would have home visitations during the day and sometimes preach at night. This pastor had two churches. He allowed me to preach at both of them. I am truly grateful that he allowed me to sit and observe the Gospel preached in a time where people didn't mind hearing true holiness and living the life they preached about. I learned from the best Bishops, Pastors, and Ministers. If you were in sin you were not made to feel comfortable and continue to live in sin. There was deliverance in the word. While in Jacksonville the pastor took me in as one of his own. He took the time and had patience with me as he continued to shepherd his flock while steering me in the right direction at the same time.

My next missionary travels took me to Ft. Pierce, Florida. Here I met another nice family, Bishop LeFleur and his family. I made a lifetime friendship with the people I met. The scripture came alive. Proverbs 18:24 "A man that hath friends must shew himself friendly: and there is a friend that sticketh closer than a brother is". We still hold this friendship today. The people were very dear to me. Another friend for life from Ft. Pierce is Ceola Kitt. The young people would follow me to hear the unadulterated word of God. Of course being young myself this brought about an even greater impact on the younger generation. Souls were saved, healed, delivered, and set free. People would give their lives to the Lord and backsliders were reclaimed.

There was another little place along the East Coast called Lake Worth, Florida. All of these were little cities the Lord would send me to. But the revivals would impact the entire city. In this little city the pastor was Reverend Nesbitt. He and his wife welcomed me with open arms. From there I went on to West Palm Beach, Florida; there were Reverend and Sister Rolle. The towns were small, but Oh the Lord met us there. My next stop would be to a little wooden church in Jupiter, Florida. Reverend Nesbitt left Lake Worth and began a church here. He asked me to come and render a service. I traveled alone during this time of my ministry, therefore I played the piano, held praise and worship service and conducted testimonials. After which I preached the word of God. I did it all with joy. I worked in these little towns during the day, then preach at night. This was done during the off season of harvesting.

After preaching on the field for the Lord, it was time to prepare for our annual trip to the north to harvest the natural crops. Although an adult, I would continue traveling with my mom and dad. We'd go up for the summer and be back for the winter. To help with the finances I tried to help out working little odd jobs once we came back home. However, I didn't stay on the same job very long. I did my job well, but at times would be in another world daydreaming. My mind was constantly on doing a work for the Lord. Then I'd begin revivals again. People called me lazy. I just couldn't seem to maintain a natural job.

I know I wasn't happy working outside the capacity of the church. I felt my best working around the church. I played the piano, sang, recited poetry, preached, you name it I did it. And that with joy. When I did it people's hearts were touched. To please people I tried the working world, but it didn't agree with me. If you know like I know that's impossible to please people. It's easier to get an elephant to roll over and purr like a kitten. I did missionary work part time, but no one considered that as an ordinary job. I just could not hold on to a full time job. I followed my happiness from the inside. I tolerated many things from the outside, but I followed my happiness. I knew what would make my spirit man happy. I now know that it is what the kingdom of God is . . . Happiness, Peace, Joy, in the Holy Ghost. I followed the peace and joy. If anything made me unhappy I took notes and tried to avoid it if I could. I tried to avoid satisfying the natural man. I soon found out that it doesn't work for me.

I had many encounters with evil spirits (demons). I didn't know much about demonic forces, but I came to know them at an early age (18 or 19). Sad to say, but I felt them most when I returned to my home. They would be more prevalent after running a revival or a speaking engagement. As I would enter the front door of my home, I could feel the demonic forces come over me to try to attack me. I didn't know what they were. I had heard people talking to me about their experiences, but I had never experienced them. I was still a child, very carefree. I had been sheltered all my life and reared in the church unexposed to many things of the world. I would go to work in the church and in revivals. But when I returned I would have to literally fight through them with prayer. The Lord would overshadow and protect me through prayer.

I remember it was around March; I was about 20 years old. I was preparing for tarrying service. This type of service may be unfamiliar to the younger generation. Tarrying service was a service to call on the name of Jesus, and you did it until you felt the presence of God and knew, without a shadow of a doubt, that God heard and accepted your sacrifice you offered up to him. I loved this service so much because this is where I first became acquainted with God as my personal savior simply by calling on his name continuously until I felt the results. There was a spirit of heaviness that came over me. This was another experience I'd never dealt with before. I began to cry and cry not knowing why. So I asked the Lord what is this? I wept continuously. Not knowing what had come over me. Little did I know I was coming face to face with death? I continued crying out to God asking what this was. I stopped my sobbing for a few seconds. Once I calmed down He began to speak to me expressing how I was feeling the effects of my father's death. Then you know I really began crying because my father and I were very close. I was devastated because of the love I had for my dad. We were inseparable and I could not see this happening to me. I got up from the altar in tears.

When I got home I was yet sorrowful with disbelief.

The next day I went to my biological mom's house. This was during the time of the Korean War. My sister, Jeanelle had moved back home with her three children (two girls and a boy) while her husband was away in combat. She lived with my parents until he returned from the war. I rode by the house and explained what I had experienced. I told her I was at the altar and the Lord told me I was moaning the death of my father. She began to encourage me by trying to make some spiritual connection to it. My mother began to say that maybe you could take it spiritually. I listened, but it just didn't settle with my spirit. I couldn't make heads or tails of it. All I know is it left me with such an uneasy feeling. I shared it with my sister as well. She and my mother began to pray with me. It brought about a little comfort temporarily. This took place in March of that year.

As we prepared to travel to Virginia, my father expressed to me that he did not want to go any further than Virginia this year. He said he had grown a little tired of the traveling. He had unrest about his traveling this year. He said he would make this his final year of traveling. He was in his sixties during this time. He felt he wanted to relax and enjoy the wealth he had stored up for us with age creeping up on him, the age of collecting his retirement. I encouraged him that was a good idea. He said, "If I could go up and come back, I'll just take it easy." I said, "Dad that sounds real good". He made plans to go to Virginia and return to Florida. So we began to prepare to leave again. But for some reason this trip was different from most. I just couldn't put my finger on it.

I was twenty years old now. I was doing much more than I normally did through all the years of traveling. We had a little over a hundred people in our crew. I would cook for the single people and my family. I would make sure we had three meals a day. My mom would do the shopping and I'd do the cooking. Many others had done it in the past. I was grown now and knew how it was done. I didn't mind helping out any way I could. This year was plentiful; the Lord blessed and prospered the people mightily. The crops were a blessing to many families in both Georgia and Virginia. When we arrived in Virginia I was excited because this is where I had received my call. I would routinely speak at various churches and do a work for the Lord. We got ready to leave and my parents had a confrontation about the journey back.

My Dad wanted to leave and head back for Florida, but my mother wanted to continue on to New York. Well, you know who won the battle. Mom was the dictator in the family. My dad went along with it for peace sake. He really didn't want to go, but being the husband and father he was he made preparations to go. My dad said to me, "I'm going on to New York". I said, "But Dad, you said you weren't going to go to New York; you were going to go back to Florida and retire and take it easy". He said, "I know, but this is a little too much for your mother to do on her own. She can't lead the crew alone. I don't want her to take them single handed". Many of the crew members came prepared only to stay until the harvest was complete in Virginia. Therefore, he had to take that crew back to their destination. I agreed to travel to New York with my mom, and wait for my dad to join us after he had taken the others back home. My brother, Lester, who no longer worked as a migrant worker consented to help my dad drive to New York and return home on the bus. He had a full time job in Sanford. There was more work on a regular time frame than in previous years work was steady, paying a suitable salary.

When he arrived in Florida many expressed the same sentiment he shared with me not to go past Virginia. They were encouraging him to follow his mind and stay. He explained to them why he had to go. He wanted to please my mother. They said he had such a strong conviction to stay, but didn't due to the circumstance at hand. He being the kind of husband he was he wanted to be there to support his wife. My brother drove him and went back on the bus. When he arrived, work had not begun because the weather was rainy and very wet. We had not begun full harvest yet. We would go out sporadically between showers. Although we could not harvest the complete crop my work was done daily because we had to eat.

I remember the Lord put me on a fast. When they weren't working, I only cooked two meals per day. So I had some time between meals. I'd get up and make breakfast and prepare for dinner. Between this meal and dinner I would go to my room and read the Bible continuing my fast. I'd just lie there praising the name of God until time to cook dinner. I had fasted this entire rainy week. I got up preparing to cook breakfast this particular morning. Every morning my dad would have the wood burning stove filled with wood and have it ready for me to cook; the fire would be hot and ready for me to do my chores. My room was right next to the kitchen. I shared a room with my cousin. I was sleeping this morning as I did all others and dad knocked on the door telling me it was time to get up and wash up to get ready to prepare breakfast. I was getting myself dressed and all of a sudden I heard a loud sonic BOOM! It sounded somewhat like an explosion. I knew my dad was in there, but I didn't know what had happened. So I opened the door to the kitchen. When I opened the door all I could see was fire, and I saw my dad run by my door engulfed with flames. I began to scream and holler to the top of my voice Daddy! Daddy! I felt helpless. There was nothing I could do. I woke up my cousin and alerted her there was a fire. My mother was across the street in another unit. She could hear me screaming and told someone it sounded like her baby crying. By this time everyone was awake it was total chaos. I didn't know what to do; I stood there frozen in shock. This was an old wood-framed two story building. The people began to run and jump out of the windows. My cousin brought me to my senses. I began to yell frantically, "How do we get out, how do we get out!" She jumped on the bed and climbed to the window opening it, and we climbed out the window to safety. Flames were everywhere. Someone had gotten downstairs and saw my dad and caught him and began to roll him on the ground. But by that time, all his clothes had burned off him. The only thing left was the thick part of his pants, his shoes and leather belt. Everything else had burned off him.

I saw him and ran to where he was and asked him," Daddy, daddy, what happened to you"? He said faintly, "I poured gasoline in the stove; I thought it was kerosene." He had mixed up the cans accidentally and happened to be standing over the stove. Some of us were standing there with him as he lay on the ground and the building burning rapidly as if it were made of straw trying to comfort him until help arrived. We were about 15 miles away from the nearest hospital. My cousin took one of the cars and began to drive to the location of my dad and with the help of some of the crew, they placed Dad carefully on the seat and proceeded to the hospital. The building was destroyed. Nothing remained but ashes.

My mom and I just walked backwards and forwards in a daze. We were all dumbfound not knowing what to do. The fire truck finally came, but they found nothing but his remains. I remember repeating time and time again, "You Cannot Take My Dad!" "YOU CANNOT TAKE MY DAD!" So we went on that day in total chaos. It was a gloomy rainy day. The grounds were wet; not fit for any activity to occur out of doors. Not knowing our right hand from our left. We sat around looking bewildered. Finally, coming to reality later that evening, we built up enough strength to go to the hospital to see my father. Many kept trying to get me to go to the hospital, but I refused. For some reason I didn't want to see my dad in that condition. I just didn't want to accept the fact that the one person on earth that I knew genuinely loved me for who I was ever since he laid eyes on me was about to leave me. I got dressed not really trying to doll my self up to be appealing to anyone. I threw on a dress, brushed back my hair, and got in the car to go to this hall of unexpected happenings. We arrived at the hospital and found out he had been burned over 90% of his body with third degree burns. He had swallowed so much of the fire that it had burned much of his internal organs. He lived about 18 hours after the fire; they had him highly sedated. We went over to see him and could see where the fire had charred his body from head to toe. The only place that had skin remaining was the place where his leather belt had been wrapped around his waist and where his boots protected his feet. It was a pitiful sight.

My life took a turn now. For I had lost the only earthly being I could receive love from without ever having to express the fact I was longing for it. I felt my world would collapse. Now my attention was totally turned to the Lord. I had gone through many horrific things in my life, but nothing could compare with this. There was a void there that could not be replaced by just anyone or thing. At this time I was engaged to a young man. He had asked my hand in marriage from my dad and mom a few months prior. I had celebrated my twenty-first birthday there in New York. He was one year younger than I was. This tragedy had left me vulnerable to get married right away to replace the void that remained. I was making plans for the wedding, but I became a little bitter. It was almost to a point of hate. I had never felt this way since I had found Jesus. All I could do was think if he had followed his mind and been led by his spirit to stay in Florida and not come to New York against his will he would still be here. There was bitterness in my heart towards my mother. We say things like this when things happen in life, but we never know. I just could not understand how God could let this happen to me. This was my first lesson in knowing that when God moves no one can do anything about it. Somehow the Lord allowed me to know he is sovereign. He does what he wants to do when he wants to do it like he wants to do it. And none can stay His hand.

I wanted to die. I just wanted to go crazy. I didn't know what I would do without my father. I didn't want to live without my dad. This was the most terrifying part of my life. The hurt the pain the agony. The thought of losing my dad. This was more than I could humanly bear. I didn't have anybody else. He was the spot that dotted the (I) and the one person in my life that helped me move on. He provided my motivation and encouragement to continue on. He was there for me when I needed someone to lean on. What would I do now?

Pulling ourselves together we accompanied the body back to Florida. My father's remains were transported back to Florida by train. This was one of the most difficult times in my life. After making all the arrangements, we had the Home Going Service. It was beautiful. There were so many family members, friends, and other relatives I didn't know existed and loved my dad. My mother and I knew we were all each other had now. Life had to move on, but somehow I could not get my life back into focus. After they put my dad into the ground I didn't know where to go from there. I stopped preaching, and that was the one thing I loved to do, but I couldn't do it. It appeared that I wanted to stop living.

After the funeral we had to go back up to New York to finish the harvest and bring back the crew. There was a large group of people to be brought back to Florida on the bus. We also had to gather the remaining supplies to be brought back in the trucks. By this time we had a bus and several trucks. The migrant life had been pretty prosperous for those that helped and us as well. It was hard work that paid off. That is the same with the spiritual harvest. Hard work which does pay off in time. "For the harvest is ripe, but the laborers are few . . ." And in my mind with the loss of my dad, I asked the question. "Now who will tend the harvest"?

I thought the only thing to do was to get married. I thought the void in my life could be replaced by a tangible source to lean on. But that fell through also. Because of our ages he had to get consent from his parents to sign the papers for us to marry. I was of legal age 21. He suggested we wait another year to marry. I couldn't wait I wanted my life to move on. I would go home close myself off in my room. I would reflect back to times when it was just my dad and me. I recalled this one incident when my mother had opened the doors of our home to some Bishops for the week and I was washing the dishes and probably daydreaming. My mother came up to me and slapped me. I didn't hear her calling me apparently I didn't hear. After she slapped me I blurted out a curse word and stormed out of the house. I walked out of the house and went into one of my dad's trucks and stayed there. After about an hour or so after he had walked up and down the streets of Sanford he decided to look in the truck and found me. We talked as only he and I could because after all we were the only ones that had to endure her domineering ways. I reflected on how much I would miss his understanding ways. I would drown myself with memories that only he and I shared. I would snap out of my other world and I would just remain isolated until it was time to go to work.

I had gotten a little job as a nurse's helper at a rest home. It was a nice little job. I was working trying to prepare myself for what was the next phase in my life, the marriage. Since that was looking bleak as well. I felt as though I had no hope.

One afternoon as I was getting prepared to go to work I had a visit from my fiancée with the plans that he wanted to wait. I got in my car and while heading in the direction for my job I wound up heading in the direction of Jacksonville. My life was in one massive chaotic state. As I continued to drive I would pass one pole after another having the mind to run into each one. The devil even had me to think of running off the bridge. I wanted to destroy everything I came in contact with. The enemy had my mind in turmoil. I had no defense for myself. As far as I was concerned my life was over. It was just one big mess. I drove until I got to Brunswick, Georgia. I drove solo from Sanford, Florida in the mindset I was in only by the grace of God crying every step of the way. I didn't know what to do next. Not knowing what I was doing neither a clue of anybody in the city. So I pulled up into the terminal of the bus station and I sat there in my white nurses uniform as if I was waiting for a bus to come. I just sat there in a daze. After a few minutes a young man came there and sat beside me and began to talk to me. This may sound far-fetched, but true. I know it was nobody but the Grace of God that kept me. I didn't know this young man from Adam. He began to talk to me. However, I can't recall what we talked about. He encouraged me to get up from there and told me how dangerous it would be for me to be there alone. I told him I could stay there.

He told me he had a friend that I could stay with. He called the young lady and we proceeded to go to her home. I got in my car and followed him to her house. She was a nice young lady. You can tell at this time I was really out of touch with reality. This was no part of my upbringing. Especially being reared in the church. God had his hand of mercy on me even in my state of confusion. She took me in and listened to my words of sorrow and wiped my tears. I explained that I had recently lost my father and my misfortune with all other plans. In the meantime I'm certain my family members were going buggy. To be honest I hadn't even thought of them. My mind was wrapped up in my own problems. I just wanted to get away. I didn't think anyone cared. But they were very concerned back home. However, I was content.

They were very nice to me. I stayed there for a while. They bought me clothes and when they ate I ate. They slept, I slept. I got a different glimpse of life. I thought I'd join the navy. I had seen this sign, "JOIN THE NAVY". I attempted to do so. I took a test and was informed that it would take a long time to get the results. I told them I had nothing but time. The application was filled out, and the process was in motion. The man implied how long the wait would be because they only accepted two women per month. I figured this was fine. It would give me time to make a conscious decision if this is what I really wanted to do. But after a couple of days they called me at my friend's house and said because I scored so high they were shipping me up to the top. They had given me a certain amount of time to make a decision.

CHAPTER ELEVEN

THE OUTSIDE WORLD

My life appeared to be at its end. My dad's death took a toll on my life. Engagement broken, I almost lost my mind nearly suffering a nervous breakdown. I was ready to do almost anything, but what I loved to do the most, PREACH! I didn't feel qualified or eligible to preach with my life the way it was. Although my scores were high to be enlisted in the navy as an officer, or rather to be trained in a higher position, I chose not to fulfill that passion. That would have been a nightmare of a move. I have a gut feeling I would have been out of the ark of safety. I made this move in haste without any thought of what I was doing. Neither did I know anything about life outside the church. I was very naive to many of life's problems and how to handle even the smallest matters. I know the Psalm came alive in my life, "Though I walk through the valley and shadows of death I fear no evil for thou art with me . . ." It had to be Rod, Staff, Grace, and Mercy on special assignment directing me on this journey I chose to take. My life appeared to be a boat lost at sea and I was very low on fuel in the middle of the ocean just drifting.

I didn't stay in Georgia long and decided to move back home. I dreaded the move, but where else could I go. I felt alone again as I did as a child with no one to love me. I became a loner very withdrawn. I just didn't want to be bothered with anybody. I thought I didn't want to live anymore. The one person I had purpose in life to live for was gone tragically. I had nobody to love me for whom I was and I was looking for help, but in all the wrong places. My mother didn't have any reason now to put up with me. I didn't know what to do.

My cousin and her family moved in with us. As much as I loved her and her family, I still felt alone. I felt like an outcast. I had to find a job to be able to live in a little peace. I knew I had to give Ma Dear all my money, but at this point I just didn't care. My life had no meaning anyway. I would come home from work give her the money I'd earned and go to my room lie across my bed and listen to my stereo. I would rely on my tapes to comfort me and I'd cry myself to sleep every night. I'd listen to Oral Roberts, A. A. Allen, and Gene Martin these ministers preached messages of deliverance. But somehow my self-pity overrode any deliverance at that appointed time. However, I do believe it was being stored up for future use. I had no one to talk to. I know the real meaning of feeling left alone. Having flashbacks of being taken away from my family as a little girl sitting on the table and my sister brushing my hair only to have to tell them good-bye. I long to have my sister by my side now just to stroke my hair and talk to me.

Somehow I pulled myself together through the remaining year of 1960. The beginning of 19 61 the call remained present in my life. I had no choice but to pull my life back together. The word was burning on the inside and I knew I had to do something to get my life back on track. The Lord allowed me to get through my grief and moments of pity, but gave me a nudge to let me know His work must be done.

I began to fast, pray, and read my word as I had before. This brought me closer to God. I'd fast and pray for months at a time. I went back to Atlantic, Virginia where I received my calling and ran a revival. This was the first time I spoke outside my home church in Sanford, Florida (Church of God). My next engagement to speak would be in Philadelphia. One of my girlfriends had gotten married and moved to Philly. She had invited me to speak at her church. Something happened that would be a life changing experience for me. Here I met a young man, and he spoke very nicely to me. But I was on a mission for the Lord. I had no time for the natural man at this time. He had told his aunt that I would be his wife. This was unknown to me. The Lord really ministered in the service. I had felt my purpose in life returning and had no time to be halted only to be let down again. I started my journey on the field for the Lord.

After I spoke in Philly I went to visit my sister in Detroit, Michigan. She was expecting her third child. This was my oldest sister who had been married for six years before being able to conceive. She was in a church service and received prayer and the Lord opened her womb. I stayed there with her and her family throughout the duration of her pregnancy. She had a loving husband and they were happily married. I left there when the baby was about 3 months old. The Lord is a man of His word. She conceived eleven children. What is impossible for man is just right for God.

We had a lot of fun with the children and reminisced about the family members and began to discuss the lives of our siblings. We lived at a distance, but we remained close. In spite of what the family had gone through we all became very successful adults.

All of the children were separated at one time or another. This was brought to my attention as I talked to my sister. I began to feel better. At least now I felt a little peace and had something to combat the enemy always thinking that there was something wrong with me for me to be the only one to have to be reared in another home. My oldest brother, Lester, at one time lived with my father's sister. As aforementioned, Annie moved with my Aunt Carrie when she was a teenager. Odell, my middle brother lived with my mother's brother in Georgia; they weren't able to bear children and reared him as their own. Jeanelle stayed home longer than most of us. Herbert was my partner as a child getting into some mischief together as a child when I stayed with my biological parents while Mom and Dad went up that summer. We had another brother, Jody. He was to Mom what Willie Mae was to Daddy. We were always close and when reunited, we never had fights as many siblings did. We were also very talented. We could have formed a singing group; we all were musically talented. I played the piano, Odelle played the guitar, Lester the Harmonica, Jeanelle sang. She sang soprano, Annie was quiet, but a prayer warrior. My dad had turned his life around and became dedicated to the church. Mom was a pretty lady and worked very hard, but many times her work went unacknowledged. The trials of life took the best of her; she began to look for love in all the wrong places. She left my dad to go to Detroit to live with my sister. She took my two younger brothers. Overall we had a hard life, but most of all we had love for one another.

After I left Detroit my journey took me to Harlem, Kentucky. I stayed there for a little over a month. While I was there I helped with the youth department and made myself available for whatever task was presented before me. Many souls were saved. While I was here I helped the minister get the church on the move. I had quite a few sobering experiences, but the Lord was teaching me. I made a few mistakes and errors along the way, but I thank God for the Holy Ghost. In Williamsburg, Virginia the Lord blessed as he usually did. I met nice people here also.

After my work was complete there I went back to Philadelphia. Here at the same church affiliation as back home, the Church of God, I was asked to speak at a program by the young man's aunt. I was still being led of the Lord. This young man had come home from the Air Force. He lived in his Aunt's house which is where I lived. I was there with my girlfriend from Florida. She and her husband lived there as well. These were new friends I was meeting. He later said when he laid eyes on me I would be his wife.

The Lord was leading me. At least I thought He was. If I made plans to do something that was contrary to what the Lord was requiring of me, the plans always flopped. Everything out of his will was a struggle for me, but when I did it the way the Lord desired it to be all was a success and ran smoothly. I would walk around in circles until I got it right. So I began to travel again and went to all the places I mentioned running revivals.

Little did I know that once your spiritual mission is complete on the road doing missionary work or evangelizing that you don't linger in a place just because you have met nice, friendly people. More damage can be done. There is a possibility you can undo what God had sent you there to mend. I learned this the hard way, but I am thankful that God is merciful and the Holy Ghost is a teacher. Remember I had no one to train me, I was a student of the Holy Ghost attending the University of Heaven. There were some classes I had to take more than once, but after taking it the second time I aced the course. I tell my young ministers things that will work and what won't work to deter them from falling into the same pitfalls. Through it all I am grateful he chose me to be a pupil, and now I am an instructor for him.

I went back home after the Lord's work was finished. I dreaded going home because things were so unpleasant for me. But nevertheless I went home and helped out with my church. This was now 1962. When I arrived home one day there was a letter in the mail from the young man I met in Philadelphia.

Enclosed in it was a ring and he asked my hand in marriage. I sent it back to him. I didn't have time for that; I was doing a work for the Lord. Somehow he caught up with me and got my address from his aunt. He was very persistent. My mind was on working diligently in the church. I was the youth leader, I worked with the choir, Sunday school Superintendent, and I just became very active working with the youth. I did accept speaking engagements, but my attention was on the church. I felt I had done my mission work on the field making my mistakes and trying to learn from them. I ministered and came back home. I didn't want to make the same mistakes so I became subject with my own church. During this process the Lord began to open doors throughout the state of Florida. My name became pretty popular. The church affiliation gave me the title of "Youth Evangelist". I worked in and out of our state office. My natural part of life was in turmoil, but spiritually it was booming. I was drawing crowds in to hear the word of God. The ministers had my name out if you wanted to draw a crowd call on Missionary Carrie Hunt. The longest I'd stay was a day and homeward bound I went. This went on for about a year.

In 1963 I inquired of the Lord about getting something steadier to help me financially. This was what I loved doing, but I wanted some skill to go along with it. I wasn't in it for the money, but I needed money to survive in the real world. So I applied to a school in Hartford, Connecticut that specialized in business and airline stewardesses and I was accepted. I went off to school at age 23. I attended school there for a year. I studied in the business field. I completed my courses and got a job in Springfield, Massachusetts at an insurance company called Monarch Life. I was very fortunate although the odds were against me; I was a female and black. There were about four blacks working with a staff of about 400 employees. It was a very nice atmosphere to work. I worked there for a year. Then my future began to look brighter.

No matter where I went, I managed to find a church to attend. While at school I was the only black attending and sharing a room with a Hispanic girl. She eventually dropped out of school and I was alone again. All the girls there befriended me. I had a personality that would cause this to happen. I also had to adjust to so many different situations all my life so it became natural to me. The room I was in was isolated from the rest of the girls. Segregation was yet alive. After my roommate left the other girls asked the housemother if I could move into the room with them. She consented and we got along well. I would do the cooking and most of the cleaning. I was older. Most of them were right out of high school. They would come to me to ask me questions, suggestions, and advice. I was like the big sister. I enjoyed this life they made me feel special. We had a very good relationship in our dorm.

While the other girls were going out on dates, meeting new friends, or going to parties I was going to church or just staying in the dorm studying. I remember one day sitting at the bus stop after class and met a young man. I knew nothing about dating or having friends of the opposite sex coming to visit. I was very sheltered and not allowed to go out on dates. I would see boys at my brother's house or slip around and try to talk to somebody. But, here I was 23 years old and knew little to nothing about what to do or how to act in this situation. My mother taught me all about housework and how to keep things neat and clean, but the male gender was never on the agenda. At my church you were not allowed to date or court as they called it. The way you got married was you saw someone you liked. He asked to marry and you were out of your mom's house. There was no such thing as a relationship of boyfriend and girlfriend. Here I was out on my own and didn't know how to build a relationship. The way I saw the girls in the dorm handle themselves with boys was my example, and I didn't see much of that.

I gave my phone number to this young man, and he began to call me. I was happy because I had no one calling me here in Connecticut. We had a nice time talking. So one day he asked me if I wanted to ride out one Saturday afternoon. I said yes, that I'd ride out with him. I readied myself following the grooming techniques taught at home and home economics class. I put on a navy and white dress that had buttons down the front and a belt accentuating the waist with my penny loafers. He arrived; I got my white sweater from hanging on the coat rack, and told the girls I'd see them when I returned. They were surprised to see me with a male counterpart. We got in his car after he opened the door for me. He was the perfect gentleman. He asked me where we were going. You know what my answer would have been. But I know he would not want to go to church on a date. With the strict church background I came from, I had no clue what the response should have been. I was not familiar with the movies, nightclubs, dinner; none of these places came across my mind. I did not know what to say. Now I know I could have said, "Let's go have a bite to eat". He suggested we go back to his place then we can decide where to go. My being naïve I said, "Okay!"

We went back to his place to decide where we could go. At least that's what I thought we were going to his place to do. He had other places in his mind that he wanted to go. I went into his house and sat on the couch. It was neatly furnished for a bachelor. He came and sat beside me. He placed his arm around my shoulders. I didn't feel comfortable at all. This was a feeling I had never felt before. I felt cornered, and it seemed like the walls were caving in on me. I didn't know what to do. He later stood over me and demanded that I unbutton my dress. It had buttons sequenced all the way down past my midriff. I refused to unbutton my dress. He began to make threatening remarks to me. I broke down and began to cry. I told him he could do what he wanted to do with me, but when he finished to kill me. I said it again in a calm monotone voice "Just kill me". I began to pray and all of a sudden I saw that demon subsided, and I ran out of the house as fast as I could. Tears were streaming down my face. I didn't bother to wipe them. When I returned to the dorm, I immediately began to wash myself. Although the Lord protected me from this near rape, I still felt dirty.

When I hear young ladies talk about date rape, I believe every word they say. I know it can really happen. Had it not been for the grace of God, I don't know where I'd be. I went on an innocent date with this young man. I thought we would go out and have dinner or just ride, and he would bring me back to the dorm unharmed. I can sympathize with young ladies who have had these experiences. It starts out innocently and then you're forced into doing something you don't want to do, you feel betrayed. You are entering this as just a friend and nothing more. You get into a place where there are only the two of you there and anything can happen. I am grateful nothing did happen to me. But from that day, you'd better believe that didn't happen again. I learned my lesson real fast. The best remedy for that is "don't be in the dark." The phrase "What's done in the dark shall come to light," the best remedy for that is: Don't go in the dark. I also remember the older people saying that one thing will lead to another. They are so right. I thank God for being a protector. He taught me a valuable lesson and didn't allow me to be hurt in the process. For this I am thankful. Me! Try that again? FORGET IT!

This experience made me very cautious and made life hard for anyone of the opposite sex to try to get to know me. If we could not communicate over the phone, there was nothing we had to say that could not be said in the midst of a crowd of people. I didn't master the relationship thing. I later told my brother about the incident, and he told me how blessed I was and that God himself protected me. He told me since he demanded me to unbutton my dress it could not have been addressed as a rape. I concluded that maybe he had experience with this dating game preying on girls of my caliber. If I had unbuttoned my dress it would have been considered consensual. My brother had gotten out of the Marines and became a policeman. He knew the legalities with these kinds of situations. He said those type circumstances aren't pretty, but that was the law. I am eternally grateful.

I graduated and went on with my profession at the Insurance Company. I began to make a life for myself. Because I had a career, my self-esteem was built up. I was finally able to hold onto a steady job. This was the longest I had maintained a job and enjoyed what

I was doing. I was now able to buy clothes and travel when ever I wanted to. I would send my mother some money; I didn't have to give her my entire paycheck. I felt good about doing it. My sister had now moved to Brooklyn, New York. I would frequently travel to visit her. I'd catch a commuter train from Connecticut and meet her in Brooklyn. One of my girlfriends had a sister in Brooklyn as well. We would do this weekly. I really enjoyed the freedom, and I was happy again.

I finally allowed the opposite sex back into my life. The young man I met in Philadelphia after an exhausting search caught up with me in Massachusetts and again asked me to marry him. We would have conversations over the phone and personal visits. I agreed, and on September 28, 1964 he won my heart. The marriage ceremony took place in Philadelphia. It was a small ceremony in a chapel with the justice of the peace. The only visitors were the witnesses for the sake of the signature on the marriage license.

I was no longer Carrie Hunt, but Mrs. James Buie. His Aunt Sadie helped us and was very sweet to us. Before I arrived for the wedding James had the apartment ready for us to move in after we exchanged vows. I informed him of the type of furniture, I wanted as I traveled there from Massachusetts one weekend. I continued to work and to commute. He stayed at the apartment and I stayed with his aunt until the day of the wedding. He had a very good job. He was a barber by trade, but also worked for Ford Motor Company. He worked for the division that made the parts for tractors. He had good benefits and the salary was great.

When we moved into our apartment, everything was paid for. I had my job with the insurance company and he had his. After the marriage he told me to quit my job. He didn't want me to work. I did not exchange words. I was a happy housewife. My job now was to do the wifely duties, and I loved doing them. Again here is the training from my youth; the cooking, cleaning, ironing, sewing, and those things associated with the home. My world was coming into focus as I had envisioned it as a child. It was a very sweet life. We would go to church together, visit my sister and her family, have picnics in the park. I was living my dream. The Lord was moving on our behalf.

Shortly after the wedding I met his mother. It was a frightening experience. And on top of it all her name happened to be the same as my adopted mom, MAGGIE. The moment I heard her voice I thought to myself, "Here we go again". Only this time I didn't have to live with her, so I thought. I wasn't the bride she chose for her son. That's how some mothers are. We want what we think is best for our children. She thought there were better choices for him to choose from back home where she came from in Benson, North Carolina. I did meet one of her qualifications; I was a church going girl, but not from her church. But she was a little too late. The decision had been made; I am now Mrs. James Buie her daughter-in-law. My new mother-in-law was a pastor of a large church in Benson, N.C. When she heard her only son had married a total stranger, without hesitation she made a special trip to Philadelphia to see this invader. Because of what I had heard about this dynamic Woman of God, I had assumed that she would be very negative. Maybe she came to check me out to see what she had to pray for.

After getting to know her, I later found out that her bark was worse than her bite. She came off as being a Grizzly Bear, but she turned out to be a cuddly Teddy. Since she stayed with her sister during her visit, we spent most of our time there. Then she came to visit our place. She stayed in Philly for a few days then went back home. I could now breathe a sigh of relief. Our lives and love continued to flourish.

I remember telling him about a car I wanted. He didn't hesitate to try to get it for me. When he went to get it, they told him he needed a co-signer. We couldn't get anyone to sign for us. We were young, newly married with no credit. The Lord made a way soon after. He worked at it until he was able to get the car I wanted. It was a 1962 blue and white Cadillac. My dream car, it was like heaven! My dreams were finally coming true. They were all happening so fast we had been married only a few months. This was still 1964. The car looked brand new. The dealer had polished it up for us; it was beautiful! And the most amazing thing about it was, we needed no co-signer. God doesn't allow anybody to share His glory. All credit belonged to God; man had no part in it.

Every Friday when he would get off work, I'd have everything packed and ready for us to travel to Brooklyn to visit my sister, or we'd visit my girlfriend from West Palm Beach who had moved to New Jersey after she had gotten married. We just had so much fun traveling the highway visiting others. We also went to North Carolina to spend time with his mother. It was no longer a frightening experience for me, but I had to watch every step I took. I didn't feel very comfortable around her at times. She had an unusual way of getting her point across to people. She was overall a nice lady. She had recently become pastor of a church that had just started. I could detect some unrest about being the new person in her life during my first visits. My actions let her know I was there for the long haul.

When we announced we were having a baby, her first grand-child, it brought about a change of heart. In August of 1965 I became pregnant. We were excited. My pregnancy was not of the norm because of a high level sickle cell trait. I think she was more elated than we were, if that were possible. She began to pamper us making sure our needs were met. At this time my husband wasn't comfortable as a barber and began to make plans to attend college to earn a degree to be able to better support our family.

He felt this was vitally important especially since he didn't want me to work, but stay home and be there for him. The next year May 26, 1966, I delivered a bouncing baby boy. We were still living in Philadelphia at the time. We lived across the street from "Father Divine". He was a very popular minister in his time with a vast num-ber of followers and was well known throughout the country. For the people of the community and other surrounding areas, this minister was a lifesaver during the depression. If you were not able to afford the necessities, he gave them to you and allowed you to make a commitment to better your education to be able to support your family. He encouraged the men to be out front and have the ability to support their families. He had a restaurant, store, and a building set-aside for the community to become better educated. This was a real example of not just giving a man a handout, but assuring he knew how to obtain it and keep it.

Now the thought of going to college was becoming a reality to my husband with the new addition to our family. My mother-in-law caught wind of this and offered to help us if we would move to North Carolina. He had made plans to attend school up north, but she presented us an offer we could not refuse. She was willing to send him to school. I also think this was one way she would be able to spoil her one and only grandson. You know the tactics parents and grandparents can use when they see you in need.

We agreed to move to Benson, North Carolina. He had been accepted to attend Shaw University in Raleigh, North Carolina as a business major. The baby (James Avery Buie) and I went on ahead of my husband, and I got a job working at the high school as a secretary. My mother-in-law kept the baby for us. He later came to move in with us after he finished business in Philadelphia. We had a bedroom in her home that we shared with the baby. We had a crib on the side of the bed where I slept, the dresser drawer and chiffonier at the other end of the bed. We were a little cluttered in the room, but happy because we had each other. James commuted back and forth to school, coming home on some weekends.

Since my Mother-in-law was the pastor of the church, I joined right in doing what I loved to do. I played the piano, sang, worked with the youth department, and spoke occasionally. This brought back memories of back home. My mother-in-law loved the people of her church and would do anything she could for them. She also was a great example for me. She became my mentor. While my husband was away, there was much time for my mother-in-law and

I to bond. The birth of the baby shed new light on our relationship. God has a way that is mighty sweet. He placed me in this situation to be trained for the preaching of the Gospel. Little did I know it at the time, but our thoughts are not His thoughts, neither our ways His ways. She was one of the best pastors you would ever want to see. She had a few faults I didn't want to emulate, but basically that was because our nature was altogether different. She cared greatly for her people.

During the breaks after each semester, Jimmy as I now called him since there was another James in the house, would travel to Philadelphia to continue to work with the car dealership. His mother was paying for his education, but there were other needs. James held on to this job because of the benefits it provided. He continued to carry the benefits for us in order to have health coverage although the salary remained the same. There were no jobs in Benson that could match the salary he made there. Benson was a farming community. He was a good provider for us and had big dreams for our future. Therefore, he did what he had to do to accomplish them. I'd stay in Benson during the summers; he would go to Philly. There were weekends the baby and I would travel to be with him. He was living with Aunt Sadie during this time.

When we weren't traveling to Philadelphia, I was driving my mother-in-law around, I didn't mind; we had a good relationship. I enjoyed working with her around the church. There were such nice people there. They made me feel like a part of them. Many of them only knew me as her daughter-in-law, but I got great respect, and I also respected them in return. While staying there with my mother-in-law, I was constantly getting pregnant. The same year we moved in her home, I became pregnant with my daughter. My son was eight months old when I discovered I was pregnant with her. I loved being married, but this was the part that wasn't too tasteful to me. I didn't mind the fact I was getting pregnant, I just didn't want to have them so close together. But I didn't know that God was doing a quick work. I was staying in His will. The pregnancy didn't hamper the routine travels by Jimmy. I thought my life was coming to an end with each pregnancy. My mother-in-law stuck right by my side, she again made sure we wanted for nothing, and that I had proper care. I cried most of the early stages of my pregnancy. My husband finally asked me one day, "Why are you crying? You act like you are having these babies by yourself?" I just didn't think I should be having them so fast. After all, the baby was only six months old, and I was now two months into my pregnancy. "He will still be in diapers," I said to myself. But God has a way of turning your dark clouds into sunshine; He made me realize, I was not in this alone. I had more than many young ladies had back then. I had my mother-in-law right there and a husband that provided for me and loved me dearly. Not only that, but the support from the church.

Back then neighbors were very neighborly. Anything they could do for you they did it, especially when they saw you trying to better your condition. So I dried my tears and delivered a beautiful baby girl on August 13, 1967.

After the birth of my daughter, Carsandra Denyce, I told my husband the room was getting a little too crowded. I had the baby sleeping in the bed between us and James Avery whom we call Avery was sleeping in the crib. There was definitely not enough room to put another crib. We were too cramped. So I suggested he find us a place to live of our own. He agreed and began to look for a house large enough to accommodate all of us. After we informed my mother-in-law, of this she didn't receive it too well. She was very domineering. The red flags began to rise; it was de-ja vue. I thought I had left this in my past. Once you got attached to her, there was no letting go. "After all I've done to make life comfortable for you, you are going to leave," she replied. She thought I was working against her. She said this was my idea. Jimmy told her this was the best thing for us, as well as her. There was not enough room for two families in the two-bedroom house. We needed to give the children more space. God worked it out. James was able to find a place in the housing projects near the college. They had recently constructed these facilities. It was brick and in the form of a townhouse. The bedrooms were upstairs and living room, bathroom, and kitchen were downstairs. They were very nice. And most of all we were able to afford it. Due to his GI benefits, he was able to get the apartment from the income of his check. We lived for little or nothing. The check he received was sufficient and provided a nice comfortable life-style for the children and me. I was happy to be able to get my furniture back and decorate the way I wanted it to be. I was a happy homemaker again. We made the right move, and it could not have happened at a better time. Again I found out I was expecting the third child. This time Carsandra was a mere four months when I became pregnant. I began to feel like a baby-making machine.

This was not the end of the relationship with my mother-in-law. I traveled back to Benson with the children to attend church. It was about a thirty-minute journey back and forth to the church services. She had the weekends and other service nights to bond with her grandchildren. The oldest child was walking and talking pretty good, and just about potty trained. I enjoyed making clothes for my daughter and myself. I would sew nice table clothes and place mats, anything to make the house look like the happy home I had dreamed of as a child. This was good therapy for me to help drown out my sorrows of becoming pregnant AGAIN so soon. Again I didn't know what God had planned for my life.

During the summer of 1968 my niece, Joette, came to visit me from Brooklyn, to help out with the children. My husband was working in Philadelphia, and I was left alone in Raleigh, N.C. My sister allowed her to come along and help with some of the household duties as I became even more enlarged. I got really depressed one day and the Lord had me to stop in my tracks. In the midst of my praying and complaining I was sobbing over being pregnant once again and the Lord began to minister to me and said, "What you should be praying for is the male child you are carrying." He informed me that the devil was trying to destroy my seed. He told me he is to be a prophet in his day to lead many nations to the kingdom. The child I was carrying wasn't so much for me, but to perform His work. He also led me to the scripture in the book of Revelations chapter12. I put emphasis on verse 5, "And she bought forth a man-child, who was to rule all nations with a rod of iron: and her child was caught up unto God, and to his throne." After I got myself together I repented and began to cry out to God concerning my baby. Then I went over to a neighbor's house and shared with her what the Lord had spoken to me. During this time there were no sonograms to tell you what you were having. My friend, Shirley, was a pastor and was expecting also. She began to pray with me as well. She lived in a place called Chapel Hill. I frequently visited her church when I didn't attend church in Benson. I prayed that I would have a healthy child and asked God to protect him. I didn't have any knowledge what God was doing or about to do in my life. But I do remember the vow and commitment I had made with the Lord. I promised to allow Him to use me any way He chose to do; only not to leave me, and I would do His will. I said it, and I meant it. I just didn't know what road lay ahead for me. But the road that leads to life is narrow, straight, and there will be few that finds it. The road will sometimes be a little rocky, but He prepared the proper shoes for me to travel this road. I can only put my trust in Him for He had not failed me yet.

I immediately repented for my actions and sure enough when my last baby was born, he was ill. He was jaundice, and was not allowed to come home. I told the doctors if I could not take my baby home, I would not leave. They allowed me to remain at the hospital and when he was well enough to come home, we came together. The doctors didn't know what was wrong with him, but they did all they could do. I did know what the Lord had told me during my first trimester. The saints and I began to pray and I believe that that was what brought about the improvements to permit him to come home. His blood count began to improve, and he was released from the hospital. I would keep him in prayer lines during revivals and regular church services; the prayers would go up for him.

I would watch my baby in his crib trying to do the things that his older siblings could do without much effort. He had great difficulty at achieving the smallest task. He would not be able to pull up in his crib as normal babies could. He just looked so weak and feeble. He just appeared helpless at times. His weight gain was a much slower process than the average baby grew. His eyes would at times become a glossy yellowish color. While the older two children would be playing with their dad wrestling in the bed and having pillow fights, I would have to cater to many of the needs of Kevin. We named him Kevin Corwin; he was born in Raleigh, North Carolina. Each of my children was born in different cities. James in Philadelphia, Carsandra in Benson, and Kevin in Raleigh each to me was as unique as the different places as they were born. They were my little world.

As time moved on and Kevin began to try to crawl he would just fall back on his little belly. I remember one revival service the Lord was really moving and the speaker was preaching under the anointing of the Holy Ghost. I wanted to enjoy the word, but I could not stop Kevin from crying. Several of the Mothers of the church tried to pacify him. Even his grandmother tried to console him. Just a mere touch to his body caused him to scream out in pain. Finally his grandmother said, "Take him to the hospital to see what is wrong with him." There is nothing wrong with seeking medical attention. This doesn't mean you don't believe what God has said. Many times you need to know what to ask God for specifically. If the problem is with his blood we don't want to be praying for his sight. We will be specific with our prayers. This will bring about unity when we pray.

Jimmy and I took him to the doctor to find out what was wrong with him. He cried the distance from the church to the hospital. I had to lay him on a pillow to avoid him touching my body. The doctor said he had a chronic illness that there was no known cure for. They said he had Sickle Cell Anemia. I had no knowledge of what he was talking about. He tried explaining it in layman terms. This disease is common among black individuals. Sickle Cell is a disease in which the red blood cells are shaped differently from normal red blood cells in a healthy person's body. The cells don't carry oxygen to the tissues, as they should. When the blood vessels branch off to the smaller capillaries they aren't able to pass through the smaller blood vessels and their shapes become more abnormal. This is where they derived the term sickle from due to its shape. In the healthy person's body the spleen will function to help filter out the improper enzymes, but his body is over working the spleen and the spleen begins to eat up the blood that would normally pass through. Due to the blood not being able to pass to the organs properly this will have him to buckle over in excruciating pain. They did not have this much information on this disease and they determined he would have a life expectancy of six years. To better give an example of the disease picture you trying to board an airplane and having to pass through the metal detectors. If you have anything on with some type of metal you are not permitted to pass. That is what happens to his red blood cells they are not permitted to pass through the spleen and gradually it will deteriorate and the waste deposits will remain in his body. Just as if you didn't pass the test to board the plane you will remain at the holding cell until you are searched and allowed to pass.

After receiving this information we left because the doctors said there was nothing they could do. They could only vaccinate and give the routine checkups. We left the room knowing the only one to be able to handle our case was God. Jimmy went out to get the car and I waited with Kevin in my arms looking up to the heavens saying God you said he was put on this earth to do a work for you. So you have to keep him I can only put my trust in you. The doctors gave him six years, but God works with extended plans, he is now 31 years old with a family of his own. God can and He will. Just trust in His word, He cannot lie.

My children were growing and we were doing well. I decided to go to work at the school again. It got to be too much for me, and I had to quit. I stayed home and became content. Just being a happy mother and homemaker. And I did what I loved most of all working in the church and traveling to Florida visiting my family to show what God had done for me with my little family. I enjoyed seeing the smiles on my children's faces as they saw the place where I grew up. My dad always made the comment about Kevin looking just like him. And he did. We lived in Raleigh for three years before the next chain of events would occur.

I prayed that God would fulfill my calling because I knew he still had his hand on me, and I had not accomplished what he had for me to do. I prayed for good health to do a work for him. I didn't realize what great pains and trials would be faced to fulfill this calling, but I was willing to be a humble and obedient servant for

Him. I personally thought," what could be more devastating than what I have already come through". I had been put up for adoption; brought up in an abusive home; lost my father to a tragic death and escaped a near rape. I enjoyed sweet fellowship but became pregnant annually. To top it off, I now had a child with an incurable disease. What more could happen?

CHAPTER TWELVE

Part 2

DEATH OF MY FIRST HUSBAND

During the last year of my stay in North Carolina, so many things were happening to me. At the same time, the Lord was trying to show me how to be sensitive to the spirit. But I didn't know neither did I understand. Consequently, He had warned me about my dad's death. Because I was so young and unlearned in the spirit, it came upon me unaware. Again he was trying to warn me about Jimmy's death. I was sensitive to the spirit, but yet unlearned in the spirit. I remember the entire year of 1970. Some things I understood and some I didn't. I always ended up in the safety zone because of my obedience to God.

I remember one night my mother was with me. As I stated previously, Jimmy was working in Philadelphia for the summer. I had pleaded with her to come and spend a few days with me. My babies were very close in age, and I was somewhat tired in my body. Before I could get one out of diapers, I was carrying another one. I loved everything to be clean and in order. So I was very fatigued and worn out. Therefore my mom consented to come and help me out.

One night, they had gone to bed and were fast asleep. For some reason, I could not go to sleep. I was just lying in my bed reading. I put the book down and tried to get to sleep. But sleep was not in sight for me. During that time, we lived in a townhouse apartment, and we had a habit of leaving the windows open upstairs. Meanwhile, I got up and went into my bathroom, but I didn't turn on the light. I sat down and saw a shadow reflection. The bathroom was directly over the back porch. As I sat there, I saw this reflection from the corner of my eye. I said no, this can't be. I stood upon the bathtub because it was directly under the window. Sure enough there was a man bent over trying to hide himself on the roof. Apparently, he was waiting until I turned the light off and left the bathroom to make his next move. Immediately, I realized that we did not have any kind of protection. We did not even have a phone. But I yelled to my mother, "Mom call the police; there is a man outside our window." When I said that, he jumped down and ran. I heard him when he hit the ground. I knew then that it was the Lord who kept me awake that particular night. Had I fallen asleep, the man probably would have come into the apartment. I kept the light on through the early hours of the morning.

God just began working things out for us. When Jimmy came in from Philadelphia, I told him about what happened. He purchased a gun for me. Of course, I had never touched a gun and certainly did not know how to use one. He showed me, but I never bothered to use it. He put the gun far back on the shelf out of the children's reach, almost out of my reach. But I began to say to God, "Lord you are my protection." "You protected me then; surely you will protect me now." "You could have let me fall asleep and allow the thief, the robber or murderer to come in, but you protected us." "You are my source." So the gun stayed just where my husband put it.

The year progressed along. I can remember as if it happened yesterday. God was preparing me for the future tragedy. My spirit became sensitive to a sound, a loud pop sound. It could be a firecracker or whatever made that loud pop sound. Kids could be out playing and if that sound came, it drew my attention. My spirit was very sensitive to whatever sound made a pop. I would just shake at that sound. "I know I am not afraid of a firecracker or that sound, why am I shaking like this?" I didn't know, but I later found out the spirit was trying to warn me for what was about to come. That's why today I am so sensitive to the spirit.

That year was a glorious time, a happy time. My life was moving and things were very pleasant. Jimmy was in his third year of college pursuing a degree in Business Administration. We had made plans to move back to Philadelphia once he finished school. Yet, there was something again in my spirit following me. It was Florida. I knew that someway, somehow I had to get back to Florida. Of course I thought it was going to be my first missionary journey evangelizing once I got back. The children were getting a little older. I remember telling my husband I had to get back to Florida. He responded by saying," Well, if you must go back, just let me know." "You know I don't mind your going." "I'll make arrangements for you to go." But I could never get a clear picture of it.

One night I had a dream that I was back in Florida. Some years ago when I was a little girl growing up in Sanford, right on the St. Johns River, a bandstand was there. They had various outdoor concerts. That's where all the entertainment was held. Across the street was the zoo where they housed small animals. We all enjoyed going there every Sunday afternoon. We all walked downtown after church to play with a gorilla. He would respond to us. In my dream, I was back in Sanford at the bandstand. I had my choir. They were standing on elevated bleachers. There were about 300 voices in that choir, and I was standing up in front of them. They were singing so until it was like an echo going up to heaven. It was such a beautiful dream. I woke up and that dream seemed to follow me everywhere I went. I would often think about this large choir, so I told Jimmy about the dream, and we both marveled. At the same time in my mind, I knew I had to go back to Sanford.

The year took on a strange turn when Jimmy returned from working in Philadelphia. It was near the fall of the year, and he was coming to get ready for his fall term in school. About 75 miles from Benson in a little town called Rocky Mount, his car engine blew up. He had called his mother and asked if she would pick him up. They had a heated conversation over the phone because she was going to send someone for him. At the time, her car was not road worthy for distant driving. I remember becoming fearful that day. The young man who picked him up found him in such a rage when he got to him. He began to witness to Jimmy and told him he had a call in his life. He wanted to know why he was running from God. Well, when he brought him home, the rage was still in him. He and his mother had words. They really expressed their anger with one another. I tried to calm both of them to no avail. By this time, his mother was hysterical. I tried to appeal to each of them individually. I said, "don't talk to your mom this way. This is bad." The man told Granny B. what he had witnessed to Jimmy. She confirmed the call in his life, and said he would not totally yield to the Lord. Because our car had broken down, we had to use her car to get back to Raleigh. Of course, they continued to have words. I specifically remembered her saying, "You will never hurt me again the way you have today". "If anything ever happens to you, Carrie doesn't have to let me know." He responded by saying, "If anything happens to me I would not want her to let you know." It even came down to the death. "If I die, I don't want her to let you know." She responded back. They vowed that day that they did not want to see each other anymore. I'm sitting there, knowingly, he was getting himself in trouble because she was a woman of God.

Although anger and hurt had motivated and controlled the conversation, I knew they loved each other. Jimmy was her only child and she loved him. They were very close. She sat there terribly wounded and bewildered. I tried to comfort her. I said, "I hope this does not include me because I'm not taking sides in this. I love both of you. I don't want to choose between the two of you." They had concluded they would not see each other again. She did not respond. She just sat rocking and crying.

On our way home I asked him why did he talk to her that way. It was very dangerous to do that. He proceeded to tell me I shouldn't want to go either the way they talked about me. But I told him that I went to church there, and I would not stop attending church. I was the musician for the church. I could not change his mind. From September to January, he never set foot over there again. Later, she came to herself and came over and apologized. They accepted each other's apology but their relationship was not the same.

I don't think she really knew the essence of what happened, but the day they vowed not to speak to each other again, she gave him up. They have had heated discussions before, but he would always become subject. From September to January 1971, those months were like a shaping point. In January he was gone, and she was again devastated. She had to give him up because of the hurt and the pain. When she gave him up, the scripture *"Honor thy father and thy mother: that thy days may be long upon the land which the Lord thy God giveth thee"*, became alive in my life. Truly, I admonish and encourage every young person regardless to how you feel, remember that scripture. Every commandment of God is true. From September to January, things were very pleasant between Jimmy and me. He had one more rage with me but thanks to God, I prayed my way through it. Several things happen in those three months: I became pregnant again, and I was in an emotional state. I remember praying to the Lord because my baby was sick, my health was bad because of the sickle cell trait I had. I believed I was too weak to even carry another child. Remembering the ordeal that I had with my baby, I didn't want to get upset so I went on a fast. I told Jimmy I'm going on a fast if it's okay with you. I need the Lord to do something for me. I didn't tell him about the pregnancy. I had gone to the doctor and talked with him. Because of my sickness and the baby with sickle cell, they would abort it because it would be dangerous for the baby and me. I didn't want that so I went to God. I remember praying, "Lord, I need you to take this case into your hand. I want you to touch my womb. I can't afford to be pregnant again. My health is in jeopardy, and I have one sick baby. My husband is in school, and we do not have a full income nor do we have the finances. I just outlined all our hardships. Then I lay hands on my womb. *"Lord if it be so, allow my womb to release my cycle and let it come normal."* Sure enough, the next morning God had answered my prayer. Had I not fasted, I would have been pregnant when my husband was killed. The Lord did this for us and I began to rejoice in the God I served.

The Lord did many things for us. He was working things out for us. We didn't know what was about to happen, but all of this was taking place between September and December. Jimmy finished the fall semester in December that year and went back to Philadelphia to work during the Christmas break. We had purchased a little car for him to go back and forth to school. It was a 1969 Rambler; I also used it for my trips to Benson. So he rode the train to Philadelphia while I prepared for the holidays. The children were 4, 3, and 2 years old. The two older ones could remember the holidays. I put up a little tree, decorated the house, then I went out to buy their toys.

One night I was leaning over the kitchen sink. By now I knew the voice of the Lord and how He dealt with me. Even though it was through trial and error. I could really feel the presence and leading of the Lord as He spoke to my spirit. I began to really know the difference. It was becoming clearer. The presence of the Lord was identifying Himself with my life. There were some things I still did not know and understand, but God was so patient with me. He is so kind and long-suffering towards us.

As I was leaning over the sink, I remember the spirit spoke so expressively to my spirit. He said, "What will you do if Jimmy never came back to you?" I answered and said, "if Jimmy never came back to me, my children and I would move back to Florida. I'll make a life for myself." But then I shook myself. I said, "Oh, but I am not worried about that. Jimmy is coming back. He will be back."

But a day or two later, my mother-in-law came over to see us. We were talking and she said why don't you leave him. Well from her indication, he was unfaithful and into some of everything. She said I was too nice to put up with that. Why don't I take the kids and move back home. I didn't know what he had done. But I just smiled and did not comment. After she left, I thought maybe I should leave, in which case, I would have to move back with my mother and find a way to care for my children. The other alternative, I could stay and adjust to what was going on and let him provide for the children. I was tossing ideas back and forth in my mind.

Anyway, when he came by, I confronted him. He denied what I asked him. Now this is how I reasoned. There is no way I would take his word over Mother's (my mother-in-law) word. If I had to go by reason of decision, I would take his word, since these are his children, then he's going to take care of them. Even though I knew she was telling the truth, these were his children; so I made a choice to stay. It was not that I believed what he said, but I made the decision to stay for the sake of the children. So I moved on. I didn't mention it anymore. Even though I knew he was lying, I never told him what his mother said. Those last days together were very pleasant. January 19th would be another dismal day for me.

I was a seamstress and took in sewing. I also made outfits for my little girl and myself. This specific day I was sewing, and I had it facing the window, something that I didn't normally do. It was early evening almost dusk. While I was sewing, I heard a knock on my door. I looked down and ran downstairs to the door. It was one of my neighbors. As I opened the door, she said breathless, "Carrie, I need you to come with me. I think your husband has been hit by a car." "Jimmy?" I said. "Are you sure that's my Husband?" She was certain it was he.

I thought he was in the back. He had come in from school and I had prepared dinner for him. He came in and asked where were the children. They were upstairs so he went up to play a little while with them. They were already dressed for bed. He would come in and play with them before I put them in bed then we would have time together. After he finished his dinner, he said he was going out to fix the car. He had bought a part for it. So that's where I thought he was.

Well, another neighbor came to be with my children. When we got there, he had been moved. We asked the police where was the young man who was hit by the car. Of course they wanted to know who was asking. I identified my self, and after finding out I was the wife, he told us he had been taken to the hospital. He had been shot. Of course, you can imagine how my heart was pounding. "Shot!" we screamed at the same time. An off duty policeman had seen him stagger and fall. He drove his car over and shined his headlights on him. Then he saw that he had been shot.

At the moment while he was working on the car there was a domestic disturbance in the house across from him. Gunshots began to ring out with bullets sailing through the air. He tried to run, but two bullets hit him in the back, and one went into the kidney and the other tipped his heart. When I arrived at the hospital, they put me in a small blue room. I didn't know what this room signified, but the ladies who were with me did. Finally, the Doctor came in and apologized and said they did all they could do. He was dead upon arrival. I was devastated! I just could not believe it!

Then I began to fear for the men I loved. Another tragedy! First my father, now my husband; then I feared for my oldest son. I could remember how I reacted when my father died. I began to plead with the Lord not to let this happen to me again. Please help me! Don't let it happen again! The rest is just a blur, but I remember lying on my children's bed saying here today and gone tomorrow. I went in the bathroom and stared in the mirror and said, "Job, I know how you felt. I feel like your sister. Let me borrow your words." I looked up towards heaven and said, "Lord though you slay me, Yet will I trust you." I remember letting him know that I feel like my whole life is on an axle and it has come to a standstill.

"There is no way I can get it turning again; but God if you want me to continue to live, then you will have to get my life turning again." This is too hard for me to bear."

There was no money because we were living off Jimmy's grants and work-study check. I had three babies and one sick with a life expectancy of six years. I said, "God whatever you want to do with my life, it's yours; I don't see any hope for it, but I commit my life and my children into your hands. You are my only hope; you are my source." From that day, I could not eat nor could I sleep. But never once would I charge God falsely. I didn't understand, but I decided I would stand still until God revealed to me or make me understand if He so desired.

Jimmy did not go without warning. I recalled the many events leading up to his death, one distinctly. One night about midnight the latter part of September, we heard a knock on the door. We both said at the same time, "Who is that knocking at this hour?" We jumped out of bed, and he went downstairs to the door. There was a lady whom the Lord had sent to warn him of his wickedness. I couldn't make out exactly what she was saying, but he did not reject what she was saying. I could tell that by his attitude. I asked him what she wanted, and he said she was just witnessing. I said, "This time of night?" He said, "Yes." But I found out later. The lady told my mother who had come to stay with me until I moved back home.

The Lord had been dealing with her concerning Jimmy, but she kept putting it off. But the night she came, she could not put it off any longer. She had to come. This was three weeks before the accident happened. She said, "Son, God is calling you and warning you. Whatever you are doing, stop it. The road that you are on is leading you to destruction. God wants you to switch it. Change now and turn. He did not reject it, but he did not do anything about it. It's very important to obey God when he gives you a command. In our disobedience, we can hold up another's blessing.

Though tragedy had struck again, one thing I knew, I loved my savior. I stood without understanding, without knowledge, but I stood in the love of my God. That was one thing I was not shaken in. I kept saying over and over, God I love you.

Those six years, God had proven himself to me in so many ways. By being there with my mother-in-law, I gained strength. For she had a ministry above ministries. She was a woman used by God, and I learned so much from serving her. Although I was a preacher, I only preached about three times while there. But I served her. I learned so much from her. I studied her behavior, her mannerism and picked out all her good qualities not knowing that God was shaping me.

The entire year of 1971 seemed to be at a standstill for me. But I determined that I would not make one step without Jesus. I told Him, "Whatever you want for my life, you plan it; and where you lead me, I'll follow." "Wherever you direct me, I'll go. For without you I can do nothing." That was my covenant. I could not live my life as Carrie any longer. Then the scripture "It is no longer I, but the Christ that lives inside," came alive. From that moment on, I knew whatever people saw in me, it would not be me, but Christ. That way it was easy to give God all the Glory. I did not live nor plan pass one day. That is how I live today, one day at a time.

CHAPTER THIRTEEN

A NEW DAWNING

"... Weeping may endure for a Night,
but Joy Cometh in the Morning...   Ps. 30:5

In 1971, I moved back to Florida in Granny M's home. My three children (ages 2, 3, 4) and I shared my former bedroom. There was no more room so the children slept in my bed, and I acquired a single bed to sleep beside them. Through the agony and pain, I purposed to use my time to bond with my children in a special way. Each day was an effort just to make it. In as much as I wanted to bury my head in my sorrow, I could not for the sake of my children. These little ones depended upon me. They were only babies. As the turmoil in my life began to cease, I devoted most of my time to my children. We did many fun things together by attending amusement attractions and by playing games with one another.

To keep myself busy, I returned to my home church, **the Church of God**, and became active again in my choir. While waiting for directions from God, I began to encourage the young people and to accept speaking engagements on Sunday afternoons. This proved to be the best therapy for me. I no longer moped around the house, but became involved in outside activities. Word spread that I was back in Sanford, and the young people began to return to the church, for many had strayed away. Many souls were saved; backsliders were reclaimed, and many received spiritual healing and as well as physical healing. The healing process had also begun for me.

After moving back to Florida, I began to establish a close relationship with my biological parents. For I never had a close relationship with them. My mother kept my children because I did not want to place them in a daycare center while I worked. This was a draw card for us. Through the years, my mother became my confidante and one of my best friends. My father, Lester, who once was a minister, shared some of his fatherly wit with me. Well, I began to fill that life was not so bleak, after all. In fact, it was my father who encouraged me to step out on faith to purchase my first home.

While staying in Granny M's home, I was putting money into the home and helping to cover expenses that accrued because of the extra people. However, God did not want me to become complacent there, nor did He want me to depend on others. One day while my father and I were sitting around chatting, he said to me, *"Carrie, instead of putting money here, you can put money in a place of your own."* He did not want my children to be exposed to the abuse that I had encountered. He had seen the abuse resurfacing, and I had begun to see it as well.

The wheels had been set in motion. I began to pray and seek God for directions concerning a place for my children and me. I needed something that was secure for them if I were to go back on the field full-time.

One morning after I had dressed to go to the store, I went to my car. As I placed my hand on the door, the spirit spoke to me and said, *"I'm getting ready to bless you with your home."* I got into the car full of excitement; the voice of the Lord had spoken. I was ecstatic- my very own home! Joy flooded my soul!

While I was driving to the store, the spirit continued to speak to me. *"Drive and when you see the home that you like and desire, I'll give it to you."* At this time, I was passing a sign that read: **"Washington Oaks Sub-Division"**. I got directions and decided to drive into the sub-division to look at the homes. My eyes literally lit up as I drove by those beautiful homes. I really liked what I saw. By now, I was one ball of excitement. I could hardly wait to inquire about these homes.

I proceeded to the office, but no one was there. Now there was a man standing outside the office. Well it wouldn't hurt to ask him, I thought to myself. I began to talk to him and ask about the homes. At the same time, I'm thinking that I will never be able to afford one of these homes. I even voiced this to the stranger. His reply was,

"Oh, you would be surprised. Why not try anyway." He told me the hours someone would be in the office.

Several days later, I took his advice and stopped by the sub-division's office. The spirit of the Lord was working it out for me. I just had the assurance everything was going to work out for me. I proceeded to fill out an application blank to be processed. I had no idea the salesman was taking note of me. He took my application and asked me to check back. I was rejoicing in the God of my salvation. I had taken a giant step. Of course the enemy was right there. Later on, I went back to check on the processing of my application. The first salesman was not there, so I talked with another salesman. He informed me that I did not qualify even though it was subsidized housing. Oh my! Not qualify? My little heart was totally devastated, but I held onto what the spirit had spoken. If God speaks something, though it tarries, it will surely come to pass.

God was yet working in my behalf. At the same time that I applied for the house, the office was short of help. The first salesman with whom I had spoken was discussing with the other salesman about someone filling the position. Well, needless to say, I was that "someone". God had touched these gentlemen's hearts. God had provided the means to secure income so I could qualify for the home. With only $71.00 per week income, there was no way I could qualify for this particular house. After getting the job, I was able to qualify for the home. God had done what He said He would do.

What a joyous time this was for me. My God had come through for me. In my first home, a job and working for the Lord; things were pretty bright, and my life was running smoothly so I thought.

Nevertheless, there was a stir in my spirit. One day Granny B called me from North Carolina. There was a young man from Jamaica, New York preaching in a tent revival. His name was Johnnie Washington, and he was coming to Ft. Pierce, Florida. I was told to go and hear him because he was very good. Well I didn't go because I knew if she were ranting over him, he must be very strict, and I didn't know if I was ready for that. I asked my friend, Ceola Kitt, who lived in Ft. Pierce to go and check him out for me. We were brought up in the Church of God and were close buddies. She went to check him out. She confirmed what Granny B. said, and told me I missed it. Needless to say, Granny called back and told me I missed the opportunity to meet him, but he would be back. Sure enough, he came back, and I went. That was the turning point in my ministry. I followed Apostle Johnnie Washington whenever I could. I had been reared in a sanctified church, but this man was somewhat different. He was totally sold out to the Lord. I would attend the camp meetings and travel to New York. It was in 1973 that I decided to move my membership from Hickory Ave. Church of God to Jamaica Tabernacle of Prayer for All People, Inc. I have not regretted the move.

Apostle Washington was one of my mentors in the Gospel. He was instrumental in helping me remove the spirit of fear that had a grip on me. Because of dominance, beating and abuse, fear was planted. Fear torments and motivates your life. The Apostle saw this and told me I could not work for the Lord with this fear. He worked on me night and day until I got rid of fear. I would do what people said. But because I feared God, whenever I had to make a choice, I would always choose God. That is why today, I am not moved by what man says, but I totally depend on the Lord for directions.

CHAPTER FOURTEEN

COMPELLING MEN TO COME

And the Lord said unto the servant, Go out into the highways and hedges, and compels <u>them</u> to come in, that my house may be filled.   Luke 14:23

I began to have a burden for souls as never before. With this burden night and day, I began to earnestly seek the Lord's face. During my lunch hour, I would go to my car, read my Bible and talk to God. I went on extended fasts. I was just not content. There were times when I would run revivals, drive back to my hometown and get home just in time to prepare for work. I knew I couldn't last doing this my way. God wanted all of me; I could hear him saying, *"I have need of thee."* I had to make a decision. Was it going to be man's job or God's job? I knew I could not lose on God's job.

Seeking God's face and hearing the Word of God, I knew that being holy is set apart from the world and unto God. If I were to be committed to God's holiness, I must say no to fleshly demands and live for the will of God. Therefore, I made the choice of God's job.

In 1974, I quit my job and went back on the field full time. *"The harvest is plentiful, but the laborers are few."* Knowing that to serve God in the fullness, I must reach out to others. With that knowledge, I began to seek God's direction. God was beginning to mold and shape me for his plan for my ministry.

My ministry began to take on a change in 1976. There was urgency in my spirit as I conducted revivals in St. Mary, GA. and Orlando, FL. The anointing of God reached the hearts of the wounded and those who were seeking refuge. Many souls were saved and backsliders were reclaimed. Even with the revivals and soul winning, there was much to be done. God had other plans for my life. He was doing great things for me, yet He did not want me to become complacent.

The vision of this great choir began to resurface. I had this vision years ago in the early part of my ministry. Two weeks after a revival in Georgia, I conducted a revival in Orlando at West Livingston Church of God. This was the beginning of the new phase of the ministry. Sister Shyrel V. Brown Mack had come to the revival in Florida. The saints had a habit of asking, *"Where are you going to be next?"* The spirit of the Lord had led Van (as we called her) to Florida, and she decided to stay. God was moving by His spirit.

He was sending help into the home because of the task that lay ahead for. Van moved into the home and cared for my children along with my mother while I was away in revivals.

Sister Van was the first of many to matriculate to Florida after being in revivals that I conducted. This was all in God's plan. In August of 1976 after a revival in Jacksonville and St. Mary, GA, Sister Ethel Nightingale Israel and Sister Joan Daniel began to come on weekends. I began to take note. Each time I conducted a revival, somebody would follow. Little did I know, God was sending in the foundation of the church. It was during this time the vision of my great choir began to materialize from vision to reality. By this time, saints were traveling from north and south.

May 26, 1977, the original Buie Evangelistic Ensemble was organized - not knowing that this ensemble would be the forerunner of the church. I was just one to follow the leading of the spirit. The charter members were Shyrel V. Brown, Mary Lampkin, Josie McCrae and myself. Each time the group met for rehearsal, new members would join. We rehearsed each Saturday in my home on Ellen Place. Soon afterwards, many more joined and would accompany me in revivals in the state of Florida.

One Saturday morning, Sister Daniel and I were eating breakfast on the waterfront downtown Sanford. The spirit of the Lord spoke to me and said, *"Carrie. I'm sending you to my elect. You will be training ministers, missionaries, evangelists and pastors."* I shared this with Sister Daniel. She replied, *"Oh, I wish I were apart."* I stated, *"The fact that you are here makes you a part".* She has been with the ministry from the onset of the church.

The ensemble began to accompany me in revivals and on speaking engagements. The first place was in Bridgeton, New Jersey, July 1977. Next place was at my 1957 Crooms High School Reunion where I was guest speaker. Shortly afterwards, I composed two songs, "Can't Hide Sinner" and I'll Bless the Day Jesus Found Me".

As the Word of God was proclaimed, doors continued to open. I began to go North, South, East and West. Sinners were snatched out of captivity. I began to seek God night and day as people began to reach out to me. There were so many needs to be met. After conducting revivals, many people would call with questions, requests for prayer and just to inquire about spiritual things. I wanted to be an effective servant of the Lord so I had to seek God constantly and always yield to the spirit. I began to steal away more to myself to be alone with Jesus. Many of the saints would say I'm going to be your member when you become a pastor. In fact, I was being called a pastor before I became one. This was far from me because evangelizing was what I enjoyed doing. I loved God's people, and I hated the adversary.

The more I sought God's face, the more He began to mold and shape me for the next phase of the ministry. He began to place a spirit of nurturing and compassion for people within my spirit. As He dealt with me concerning His heritage, the messages that came forth took on a different tone. In Taft, FL, December 31, 1977, I preached, "Wake Up; it's Almost Midnight". Many came to the altar crying out to God. After this service, many people followed the ministry.

January 28,1978 in Fernandina Beach, FL, the ensemble and I were asked to do a live broadcast. The message was "If I Had But A Crumb, That Would Solve All My Problems". Souls were blessed and witnesses responded that their needs were met over the airway. This was an eight(8) o'clock a. m. broadcast. That afternoon, we rendered service at another church in Jacksonville. When we arrived at the church, It was full with standing room only. The pastor of the church kept turning around to stare at the ensemble. Each time he did it, he exclaimed, "My, my, you all have been with Jesus!" The Glory of the Lord radiated all around them. One of the stipulations for being a part of the ensemble was to fast and seek God. One had to be committed to soul winning. We were doing a great work for the Lord.

During the same year, Apostle Johnnie Washington returned to Florida with the Big Gospel Tent Revival. The ensemble was well established and singing under the anointing. We were asked to sing and to be ushers for the tent revival. What excitement! To sing before hundreds! We did not have a clue as to what was about to take place. We were just happy spreading the Gospel of Jesus Christ and rendering praises unto God.

Now, we had been singing several nights at the tent. One of the ministers who were part of the tent crusade had been observing the singers. He asked one of the ensemble members about her church because he wanted to come and conduct a revival. She informed him that she was no longer attending her church but was traveling with the evangelist. For the group would come to Sanford each weekend for rehearsal and to study the word of God. Well, this minister told to Apostle Washington that the members of the ensemble did not have a home church (the members had one but were not attending). The apostle said nobody was going to sing behind him without a home church.

Apostle Washington was a man of spiritual wisdom. He saw what God was doing in my life and witnessed that I must surrender to the Lord with a yes to Pastoring. The souls who were following the ministry needed to be nurtured and cared for by a shepherd. *"How can I do this; give up evangelizing?"* I said to myself. Evangelizing was the essence of my life. I just did not see myself as a pastor. Well, we continued on the field tearing down strongholds of Satan.

The promises of God are true, but with every promise there is a condition. I had adjusted to the vicissitudes in my life; however, this one change (from evangelizing to being a pastor) I was just not ready to accept. I was content to proclaim the Gospel of salvation to the unsaved. Signs, miracles, healing and deliverance from evil spirits accompanied my ministry. Compelling men to come was what I loved. I was just not ready to yield to that little still voice, *"if you love me, feed my sheep"*. I had really wanted to go into the hedges and highways to compel men to come. Deep down within my spirit, I knew that I must die to myself and yield to God's bidding.

CHAPTER FIFTEEN

MY STRUGGLE WITH CANCER

"...Many are the afflictions of the righteous..."

One night in Newberg, New York during the latter part of 1977, I had just finish a revival service. God had moved in a miraculous way. The group was sitting around the table discussing how the Lord had blessed. The group and I had settled into the kitchen. We were sitting around the table having a snack and discussing how the Lord had blessed in the service. I remained with them for a little while and then retired upstairs. I remember going upstairs and getting ready for bed. As I lay on my bed reminiscing about the service, I suddenly touched my breast. I felt something unusual, so I began to examine my breast. This was something that I was not accustomed to doing. I mean we are told to do this from time to time, but you know how we neglect to do this. We are always thinking this will not happen to "me". For some reason, this particular night, I began to examine my breast. Sure enough, there was a lump. At first, I tried to ignore it. I said to myself, *"No, **this can't be!"*** Then I became more curious. I examined both breasts like we are told to do by the doctor. I exclaimed, "My Lord!" It was a lump about the size of a pea at that time.

Fear gripped my heart before I knew it. ***"Oh no! This can't be happening to me!" I had to calm down.*** Oh this is just a trick of the enemy, I thought. Knowing that God is a healer and a deliverer, I would not let this shake me. The fact that God is a healer was there from that day forward in the back of my mind. I was looking to reexamine my breast any day, and it would be gone. I had that confidence. I was not casting away my confidence. I knew God would stop by as he had done before. He had never failed me. Whatever I desired of Him, he granted my petition. He may not do it when I asked, He would always show up and give me what I needed. So, I didn't worry too much. I said, ***"God, you are going to deliver me, and I know you will because you are a healer."*** I just figured the enemy was using this as a diversion to distract me from the needs of the people crying out in revival.

I finished the revival and went back to Florida. I continued the self-examination thinking the lump would be gone. Yet, it was still there. Finally, I made up my mind to go to the doctor. There certainly was no need to play with this. "Perhaps it's not even what I think," I rationalized. " Lord where are you?" "Why aren't you hearing me?" All this was going on in my mind. Fear was trying to get a grip on me again. Certainly, as I expected, the lump was still there. After the doctor talked to me, he went out. I broke down and began to cry. I said, *"God, I know this is not happening to me."* Sometimes in our darkest hours, we seem like we are all alone, but God is Omnipresent. There was a born-again believer, who was a nurse working in the doctor's office. I did not know she was a believer until she began to minister and to encourage me.

When I left the office, I was thanking God for having someone there to give me a ray of hope. The doctor did not want me to procrastinate, but he wanted me to go into the hospital within a couple of months. In as much as there was a history of breast cancer in my family, this was too serious to wait. By my sister having a mastectomy, the doctor did not want me to put this off any longer than I needed. Despite what the doctor was saying, I still had the confidence that God was going to heal me.

I continued preaching the Gospel even though it seemed the clock was ticking against me. The lump in my breast continued to grow. I became a little apprehensive since it was almost a year since I had first felt the lump. *"Lord, you have not stopped by to see about me,"* I moaned. I continued to fast and pray. I told my mother and a few saints to be in prayer with me. *"Lord, something must be wrong. You have not stopped by to see about me. I can't continue to play with this thing. I know you are a present help in the time of trouble."* Each week, I was getting very serious about it. At last, I went back to the doctor.

I never cease to marvel at the ways God uses to get our attention. Before going to the doctor again, I said, 'Maybe the doctor will tell me it is gone." "Yes!" "That is exactly what he will say, I continued in my thoughts". He examined me and told me it is there; now he will tell me it is not there. I said, *"God, you just wanted the doctor to know that you are a healer. With his medical knowledge, you just wanted to confound the wise."* The Lord just let me continue to rationalize. Well, you guessed it. The doctor told me the lump was still there and growing. I needed to make haste because it was enlarging faster than it should. Satan was trying to take me out, but my God had everything in control.

Well, I told the doctor to schedule the surgery. While lying in the hospital bed, I asked God, *"Why aren't you hearing me?"* I know my faith had not failed me. *"Why aren't you answering me?"* His reply was, *"When you hear me, then will I hear you!"* Immediately, God had my undivided attention. I surrendered with a resounding YES! The tumor was removed, and the biopsy proved that it was benign. What could have been tragic for me, God turned it around when I surrendered to His will to pastor.

So the Apostle's insight was on target. On November 17, 1978, three days after being released from the hospital, seventeen of us took a stand for the Lord. We were fellowshipped into the **Tabernacle of Prayer for All People, Inc.**, Fellowship as the **Sanford Tabernacle of Prayer for All People, Inc.** The chartered members were Carrie Buie, Carsandra Buie, Shyrel Vanessa

Brown, Joan Daniel, Sharalyn M. Daniel, Lorenzo and Janice Dixon, Rutha Christian, Rosa Lee Hunt (deceased), Carrie Mack, Ronald Nathan, Ethel Nightingale, Elzata Rivers, David Sheppard, Wilma Sheppard, Rosa Williams and Triphonza Williams.

We were so excited! The members cried and shed tears of joy. Many had counted up the cost. Before we took the stand as a group of baptized believers, several of the saints who are still members were traveling back and forth each week from Jacksonville. Sister Daniel and Sister Minnie Martin were traveling back and forth together. They really wanted to go to Ft. Pierce to take the stand, but felt this was a giant step to take. There were many doubts in Sister Martin's mind. She thought she must travel to New York for church. Well, Sister Daniel said she fast for a week and seek God's face. If she were to be part of this move, she would get her answer. It was in the plan of God for her to be there. She and her daughter took a stand. She counted up the cost! Sister Martin joined later but is no longer a member.

February 17,1979, I was ordained as Pastor of the Sanford Tabernacle of Prayer for All People, Inc. under the late Apostle Johnnie Washington in Riviera Beach, FL. It was now official. I was a **PASTOR!**

CHAPTER SIXTEEN

A NEW ERA – PASTORSHIP

"... If You Love Me, Feed My Sheep..."

Jesus description of believers as lambs and as sheep implies three things: 1) a need for continual pastoral care; 2) a need to feed constantly upon the word and 3) since sheep are prone to danger, a need for repeated guidance, protection and correction. The sheep that had strayed into Sanford and my home needed to be nurtured and protected. God had been preparing me for this task all along.

Shepherding God's flock is no ordinary task. He instructs His leaders and gives them specific requirements. After I was ordained a pastor, I sought God for directions concerning His people. I learned at an early age to pray for directions. I knew that difficult days lie ahead, but with God on my side, I could face them optimistically.

The first service was held in my home on Ellen Place after we had been ordained as a church. What a time we had at our first service! We were crammed into that small living room. However, with the joy of Jesus surging in us, it did not matter. God met us there and overshadowed us with his spirit. He also confirmed some things to us. As He was speaking about what He was going to do, He was giving a vision to one of the saints as how He was going to add to the church.

At the next gathering, we organized and set up our various departments. We filed our charter in Tallahassee, and we were now ready to do a work for God. We continued to have service in the home, and at the same time prayed for a place to worship.

As visitors began to come, we overflowed the space in the living area. We put the children in the den to make space for the visitors. More souls came to be part of us. The living and dining area was too small to accommodate the people. Word spread as to how *'those people'* are *'having church!'* Still, we needed a bigger place to have church. We went back to God in prayer for a place to house the people. Prayer was the power to pull everything together successfully, and it still is today.

Our prayer was reaching the throne. One day someone told us about a church on 16th Street. I inquired about it, and the pastor agreed to allow us to share his church. We began to have services there. Well we had a few services in his church until he tried to discredit what I was preaching. I was preaching nothing but the unadulterated Word of God. He got up and tried to correct me before my members. I stood and walked out. The members followed. One of the members began to pray and ask God not to hold it to him but have mercy. "Put out of the Synagogue." That became one of our sayings: 'put out of the synagogue'. Certainly God doesn't want us to go back in the home, I thought. Nevertheless, we went back to regroup.

Meanwhile, I proceeded to establish a church. The church is the only place totally committed to keeping faith alive in the hearts of God's people. Faith comes by hearing the Word of God. How can they hear without a preacher? The adversary was not going to make me run with my head buried. As a leader, I had to keep the spirits of the people lifted. I was the front person; the point man as it is called in the military. Therefore the spirit of failure never entered into my being. We had only encountered another problem.

There are two reactions to a problem - a negative and a positive. We chose the positive. We fasted, we prayed, and we rendered praises unto our God.

This was the first of many problems dealing with man. I learned in the early phase of my ministry that it is better to obey God than to sacrifice. There will be many obstacles the enemy will throw in your path, but you must totally depend on God for He will see you through.

CHAPTER SEVENTEEN

THE FISH MARKET EXPERIENCE

"... And I Will Make You Fishers of Men..."

On 13th Street in Sanford, there was a little green building that was used as a Fish Market. It was vacant and just sitting there. My trustees and I inquired to see if it were available for leasing. It was! Our first place that we could call our church! You would have thought we had acquired a glass cathedral the way we carried on. Oh, but we were praising God for what He was doing for us. God had smiled on us. The little group seemed to draw strength from just seeing God work for us. ***Wait on the Lord, and He shall strengthen your heart.***

We started cleaning and fixing that little building with its cement floors to make it a place of worship. There was a little small room that we used as an overflow for the children in order to accommodate our guests. In addition to the small room, there was one even smaller. This very small room, wit a curtain for a door, was used as my study and to count money. Our services were certainly anointed, so we frequently had visitors.

God added to the church such as should be saved. We had only one small bathroom for both male and female. To top that off, we had two ugly poles in the center of the floor, which took up space, but we still thought it was a gorgeous palace. We were so grateful. We let God know it. We were in that little building every chance we got rendering praises unto him. We had three-day shut-ins, prayer services in addition to our regular services.

We could never erase the smelly stench of fish, but it did not matter to us. The anointing was so prevalent in that little green cement building. When people came through the door, they came in praising God! Because our space was limited, the chairs had to be folded when someone danced under the anointing. Many people came to know the Lord in the pardon of their sins in the *'fish market'*. The choir sang under such a heavy anointing until souls would run crying to the altar as the Voices of Tabernacle ministered in songs. Couples who were not married and living together gave their lives to the Lord. They separated until they married.

We didn't have a set order of service. Our services were subject to the leading of the Holy Ghost. By that, I mean if the Lord desired the word to come first, that was the order, or if the choir

160

was to minister in songs, that was the order. One Sunday during an anointed Service, the Lord was pouring out of His spirit. The group was still traveling from Jacksonville each week. In fact, Sister Daniel would travel to mid-week service on Wednesday nights alone and return the end of the week to help with the needs in the home. This group was a part of the ensemble so they had traveled the miles for awhile. This was such a faithful group of people so God wanted to do something special for them.

During this particular service, we had a word directly from the Lord by way of prophecy. The Lord began to speak to me, and I shared it. *"Because of your faithfulness to the ministry, I am going to bless you with a church in Jacksonville. I give unto power to tread on serpents and scorpions and over-all the power of the enemy: and nothing by any means shall hurt you."* Tears of joy were shed. What a time we had that day! Some had to be carried to their cars after service because they were so high in the spirit. God had once again smiled on us.

For about two years, we continued to have service there even though we were literally bursting at the seams. Many people along with their children had come to join the church. We just did not have the space. The children had to sit on the floors in the back-room because we needed the extra chairs. We spread quilts on the cement floor for cushion. The children did not mind one bit. They thought of it as an adventure. As the church flourished in the fish market, the need for a new facility became very apparent. The members stood around the walls to provide seats for the visitors.

Now, my ministers, deacons and I began to look over the city to see what land was available to build a house for the Lord. We looked at land near Crooms by Academy Manor, but that was not it. We also looked at land on 18th Street. We even considered 20th Street and Southwest Road by the railroad tracks. After investigating the building owned by Food Fair on 25th Street, we came to the conclusion that God must have the place just where *He* wanted *His* church. For we had looked into many situations to no avail.

Meanwhile, Sister Ingrid Nathan, who is our organist, shared with her husband, Deacon Ronald Nathan that she and her mother, Mrs. Cleo Burton, owned property across the street from the fish market. He asked me if I could use the property although it appeared small for a church building. Immediately, it agreed with my spirit. *"That's it!"* I exclaimed. This was part of the vision. I asked Deacon Nathan to talk with his wife and her mother to see if they would sell. Deacon Nathan proceeded to speak with them. Sister Nathan was happy that the land was suitable. As she considered what to do, she told me she wanted her mother to get whatever price she desired; so that the church could be built faster, Sister Nathan was willing to donate her part. She was willing to pay off any liens or taxes in order that the church would not have the expenses. Consequently, she asked the Lord to prepare her to offer the land free and clear. She did not want to miss it, desire it or look back in any way. She wanted to be a cheerful giver. Therefore, to be sure the Lord was speaking to her, Sister Nathan and her husband went on a fast. After the fast, they joined hands in prayer and knew in their hearts, God had said yes. God was yet providing means for houses to be built. First my home and now a house of worship for him! *To God Be Glory!*

162

CHAPTER EIGHTEEN

BUILDING A HOUSE FOR GOD

EXCEPT THE LORD BUILD THE HOUSE

"...Moved into the New Church in
Ten Months from Start of Building..."

In June 1979, we received the deeds to our new property. Another victory won. God was not letting me fail, but was helping me to meet the goals he had set before me. I was criticized, scorned and talked about. ***"Where does that little lady think she is going that small group of people?"*** We were the talk of the black community. We had escalated from 17 to 42. We may have been small in number, but we were strong in faith.

163

We didn't know anything but to believe God, fast and pray. So we went down in sackcloth and ashes for we needed a plan for our building. We continued to glorify God to render services to other churches. Some of the places were Eatonville, Taft, Hobe Sound, Jupiter and Ft. Pierce, Florida. We were known as the church on wheels. God was meeting our needs with a need. As we continued to obey God, He continued to bless us and provide finances, also.

It was during this span that I decided to get someone to assist me in order to keep the doors of the church open while I was away. One of the members of the Buie Ensemble continued with the church after it was organized. Eventually her husband joined us. He was a minister and very faithful so I decided to make him my assistant pastor. That was one of my biggest mistakes. He was influenced by another member to have secretive men's meetings. He (the instigator) did not like the way I was doing things so they would call the apostle in New York. In the meetings (I found out later) they were conspiring against me to try and remove me. I guess because I was a woman, small in statue, they felt I was a weakling and a push over. I really can't tell what they thought, but I do know they were not replacing me or calling me in question. I was called to pastor by God, not by man. He managed to attract a few supporters but in the end, he had only about three.

Well, they decided to have a meeting with the church family to which I agreed. I let them speak, and I heard them out. Since I was the one called into question, I let them air out their grievances. After they finished, I took the floor. I told them not to ever call me in question again. I am the Pastor of Sanford Tabernacle of Prayer, and I receive my instructions from God. I told an usher to stand by the door. I said you don't have to touch the door. The usher will hold it for you. You can imagine what happened next. I relinquished him from his position. Since that time, I have never had another assistant pastor. Eventually, he left and so did his followers. I was the one responsible and accountable for the souls of the people. God was giving me some hard lessons in Pastoring, but I caught on very fast.

In any organization, there is always someone who does not go along with what you are doing. The adversary will see to that. But as a leader, one must take charge and perform in love. Most leaders abhor confrontations, but know without a shadow of a doubt you will be confronted. You must seek God daily to handle such matters. You may not be able to handle them in the aggressive manner in which I did, but you must handle these types of situations.

One of my ministers was very gifted in drawing. After the Lord gave me the fore plan for His house, I presented it with Minister Robert Robinson, and he drew the blueprints for the church. Now, Robert had a friend, an architect, who put the seal of approval on it. We did not need to go to the world for much. God had people placed in our midst to carry out what He wanted done. We had carpenters, brick layers, plumbers, etc. I could relate to Solomon when God instructed him to build a house for Him. I have learned that God backs up everything that He says if we obey.

Purchasing our permit was our next phase. This was another battle. The enemy was determined not to let another church be erected on 13th Street. This street seemed to be his sole territory so to speak. He was determined no more of His was coming on the Lord's side. During the days before Sanford Tab was erected, 13th Street was a haven or should I say the enemy's ground for lost souls. Every evil work imaginable was on 13th Street.

Well, we begin our battle with City Hall. Each time we went to City Hall, we were either turned down or the meeting was adjourned without our being heard. Know what happened next? **Back to the drawing board!** You guessed it! God reassured me that our church would be built on 13th Street. We had come too far to give up now. If Nehemiah had given up when opposed with adversity, the wall would never have gone up.

God had someone in City Hall just for us. He was still giving us favor with man. (One of the councilmen at City Hall knew us; he used to be our coach, but we did not know we would come in contact with this councilman.) We said we would go back and give it another try. Before the meeting began, we were standing outside polishing up our presentation. The councilman came up and recognized us. We chatted, and he wanted to know what we were doing there. We explained to him what happened each time that we came, and what we wanted. He told us no problem. He would take it from there. When the meeting started, and it was time for our item on the agenda, the councilman just sent it through. We could hardly believe it! The question was asked of someone in City Hall, how did we get a permit? His response was "man don't ask me 'nothing' about that church." **If God be for you, who can be against you!**

"Through hard trials, tribulations, persecutions,
I'll be faithful,
I'm going to see the king."

We were singing praises unto God for the victory. He had proved faithful to us again. **To God Be the Glory!**

Now I started making plans for our groundbreaking service. I scheduled it to be an afternoon service at 4:00 p. m. The day before groundbreaking was extreme excitement! With much anticipation, we finalized everything and retired for the night. The next morning, the sky was overcast with dark ferocious, looking clouds. Thundering was rumbling and lightening flashed across the sky. The saints were anxious. Some had gone by the property and called me. One of the members called me and said, "Mom (most of them called me 'Mom') 13th Street is flooded! People are riding by laughing. They had already branded us as a bunch of crazy people. Now 13th Street had never flooded. It rained so much until there was a flash flood. Still, I said go on with the plans. Place the shovels, and rope off the corners. I turned my face towards heaven and prayed. I reminded God of what He said. It would be a groundbreaking. I believed Him. We had been an obedient people to Him. Whatever he told us to do, we did it. Sometime in the service, He would have us to go in-groups of ten and march around the property. We had shut-ins in the fish market. We sanctified that lot unto the Lord. So we knew that God would not fail us.

About an hour before the ground breaking, the dark clouds cleared the sky, a brilliant sun appeared, and the waters dried up. The sky was a beautiful blue, which was a sign that God had smiled

on us. We continued to magnify the name of **JESUS!**
"...What manner of man is this!
For he commandeth even
The winds and water,
And they obey him." Luke 8:15

As I think back, I recall three other incidents about the weather. I had to go north one year, and the weather was record breaking cold. I remember praying and telling God I just didn't want to go in that weather. He told me to go out and stand, face the north and tell him what I wanted Him to do. I did and prepared to go north on the train. When I got there, the weather had switched to record breaking warmth for that time of year. Another incident was the floods. The state of Florida was having floods just about in every city. God told us to pray! We were spared. Then there was the tornado in Sanford. Mostly every church on 13th Street received wind and hail damage. Sanford Tabernacle was left standing with no damage. When hurricane Hugo was headed on a straight course toward Florida, God stalled the storm in the Gulf; then it changed courses. Even with the fires raging all around us, God spared our homes.

We began building in September 1980 and dedicated our church debt free February 28, 1981. **He said He would and He Did!**

After the dedication of the church, I left to get some rest and to get married. I met the enemy head-on. There were dark days, which lie ahead for the church and me, days that devastated my life and the lives of those that were close and dear to me. These memories are too painful to recall, but will be revealed later with a sequel titled, "My Encounter with the Enemy."

CHAPTER NINETEEN

JACKSONVILLE CHURCH

"...Because of your faithfulness..."

After moving into our brand new edifice for the Lord, we were ready to render praises and thanksgiving unto God. Oh what joy flooded our souls! The Lord did not want us to become complacent because "other sheep of the fold, them too must I bring." Before God's master plan began to unfold, a group of faithful followers traveled the miles from Jacksonville to be in service in Sanford. These young people first started as a group of singers known as the Buie Ensemble, the forerunner of the Church. Little did they know what God was doing in their lives. However, they

169

knew to obey the spirit of God. Persecution, ridicule and abuse did not separate them from the Love of God.

Once I started my role as pastor, the ensemble was no longer needed but became the Voices of Tabernacle. Such love, joy and compassion flowed as the enemy intensified. It was a battle, but this did not deter the determination of this group of young people. They were ridiculed and accused of being part of a cult. Some even received physical abuse and was locked out of their homes after returning from a glorious, anointed service. The blessings received from the Lord were enough to sustain any blow the enemy had for them.

It was a glorious time for the saints when the Lord smiled on their faithfulness. A church in the Jacksonville area would be established for them. This ministry was the one God had assigned to them. Granted, there were other churches in Jacksonville, but all of this was in God's plan for us.

CHAPTER TWENTY

BLOOD, SWEAT AND TEARS

Many of them endured stressful situations. Some had unsaved husbands who did not understand the ways of God. One experienced a broken nose; another endured being burned with cigarettes on various parts of her body; just outright physical abuse. We were having a service one night in Jacksonville, and one of the husbands came to the church and pulled his wife outside and hit her in the eye just because she came to church. It was a trying time for the saints. They were not persuaded to turn their backs on the Lord. One of the saints had to endure having her clothes thrown out of the house and being locked out when she came home from church. One was told she had to choose between the church and her husband. It was not that she was neglecting him, he just did not want a sanctified wife. He considered us as crazy people.

"Blessed are they which are persecuted
For righteousness' sake:
For theirs is the kingdom of heaven."

Our first service began in the home of Sister Joan Daniel. We had service in the home on Thursdays, and on Sundays, the saints came to Sanford. The Thursday night services consisted of Bible Study and prayer. God set His approval by saving a soul and adding to the church the second week. Sheep begin to beget sheep. As time went on, we increased until we needed to move from the home again. We needed bigger quarters. We tried to solve our problem tentatively by moving from house to house. This did not work for long. We needed a more stable environment.

He never failed me yet; he never failed yet;
Jesus never failed me yet.
Every where I go I'll let the whole world know
Jesus Christ never failed me yet.

A door was opened. God was still providing for the faithful. We held services at St. Peters A. M. E. Church on Lee Street. Although it looked like we were about to follow the same pattern as we did in Sanford, but it didn't matter to us as long as the Lord was leading. That was a little wooden church with wooden floors. We had some glorious times in that little church.

CHAPTER TWENTY ONE

OUR WILDERNESS EXPERIENCE

Soon, from the little white church, I took the congregation to Sherwood Square on Soutel Drive. This was an old defunct Shopping Plaza. At that time there were only three other occupants in the plaza: the manager, a shoe repair shop and a laundry mat. At first, we occupied the huge Grant Dept. Store Building. I had visions of what I could really do in that huge building. But I soon found out that wasn't what God wanted. We worshiped there at that plaza approximately five years in four different locations - from the front to the back, to the side, and back to the front. Apparently, this is not my area, I thought within myself. What is happening? Why isn't the fulfillment of God's promises taking place? I know the blessings of victory, inheritance, abundant provisions, peace and rest come to the people of God as they obey Him. So, what is happening, Lord? God began to put a stir in my spirit. I began to look at property to begin building a house for the Lord. Even with thinking of building a house for the Lord, I was not satisfied in my spirit. Before we left the homes, God had already impregnated my spirit with Live Oak. I began to realize that He had placed more than just Pastoring on me. I was a builder! Before I could settle with one group of people, He was sending me elsewhere. Now, I realize I was to go and establish the churches and hew out the ground for the other ministers within the church. Being newly married, I made some mistakes through this trying time. That is why it is so important for leaders to hear God and adhere to His directions concerning His flock. Nevertheless, I'll get back to the issue at hand.

I would go into the Live Oak area accompanied by some of the members on Saturday to have prayer and Bible Study. One of the members had come from Live Oak so we would meet in her Sister's home. So I realized my calling was greater than I envision at first.

With the urgency I had in my spirit to build a house for God, I was sidetracked into buying a worthless piece of property that to this day, I have not been able to do anything with it. Just a piece of swampland - a dump!

As I previously stated, we were in several locations in the plaza. God began sending in the souls to be nurtured. The enemy began to sew seeds of discord. The once faithful little group of people began to get slothful. They were not faithful to their commitment to God. We began to wander. It was back to the homes! We did not stay long, however, just temporarily. I had to seek God's face for new directions and to see why we were out of sync with Him. One thing about having service in the homes, we were so compacted-about in there until there was no space for strife, animosity and envying.

One day while praying and seeking the lord, I felt within my spirit, it was time to move forth. I instructed my church clerk to call some Realtors in the community to inquire if there were any churches for sale. God had just the place - a union hall on E. 27th Street! The Realtor was a union hall member, and he knew they would be building a new hall soon so he took me to see the building. The minute I set foot in the building, I saw the walls coming down. The vision began to focus. **Glory To God!** I felt the peace of God in my spirit and knew this is where He wanted us.

The blessings of God began to flow. We moved into the building. The church occupied the downstairs, and the union occupied upstairs. A homeless man was living in the building at the time as a watchman for the union people. He remained for a short while for when the spirit of God occupied the building, he was no longer needed, and the union found him other quarters.

We used the building debt free for a complete year until the union hall moved out. We did not pay rent, water or light bill. We even had janitorial service. Whatever needs arose they were met.

We had time to search out lending institutions before purchasing the building. We went to several places. I remember there was a certain bank on Main Street. My secretary and I went to inquire about a loan and to fill out an application. The man was very rude and nasty to us. There was no cause for his attitude. We did not provoke him! I was irate with that spirit. But my fight was not with the man. I was very cordial, and we left. I was reminded of 'Jesus and the fig tree', and 'greater works shall you do in my name'. I left the bank saying you will not do business in this neighborhood. A few months went by. I did not give it another thought. One day we were riding on Main Street, and my secretary said, *"Look! The bank has gone out of business!"*

We are forever indebted to God for His many blessings, miracles, delivering and keeping power. For he has blessed us with a beautiful edifice with classrooms, a baptistery, fellowship hall and living quarters for the Pastor upstairs in the church. One would never know this was a union hall from the appearance.

CHAPTER TWENTY TWO

CHURCHES BIRTHED FROM THE MINISTRY

In the churches, there are talented and gifted people. I am reminded of the day on the waterfront when the spirit of the Lord spoke to me and said I would be training minister, evangelists, pastors and teachers. Many churches sprouted from this ministry. Some chose to go their separate ways. Nevertheless, they were birthed from this ministry from Sanford Tabernacle of Prayer for all People, Inc. One of the pastors moved back home to Woodbine, GA. She heard me minister at her Bible School graduation. She came to Florida looking for the church and started attending services with us. When she moved, she was not a pastor, but felt the Lord was

177

leading her in the direction of Pastoring. Our late Overseer, Apostle Johnnie Washington, placed her under my watch care. Elder Doffie Silvia is the pastor of **Woodbine Tabernacle of Prayer.**

Live Oak Tabernacle was hewed out as I was establishing Jacksonville. Because I was not able to go in and out as I desired, Apostle Washington advised me to turn over the pastoralship. **Daytona Beach Tabernacle** and **Melbourne Tabernacle** were birthed from this ministry but are not under the auspices of this fellowship. Then there is **St. Augustine Tabernacle** of Prayer with Elder William and Evangelist Yvette Montgomery. The newest church is our **Stuart Tabernacle of Prayer** with Elder Roy Stevens as pastor.

Elder Ethel Israel was a pastor among the flock. She was birthed right in this ministry. God raised her up and called her into pastoralship. She is Pastoring in Kingsland, Ga. And is doing a great work for the Lord. She is independent.

Among the flock are pastors, evangelists, ministers, and teachers who will be coming forth in the fullness of time. One of the greatest thrills of my heart is to see my eldest son come forth in the ministry. God has called him into the ministry, and he will be ordained as an Elder this year and will succeed me as Pastor of the Jacksonville church.

CHAPTER TWENTY THREE

TESTIMONIES OF THE SAINTS

DEACON AND SISTER NATHAN'S TESTIMONY

As the church began to flourish in the fish market, the need for a new facility became very apparent. We had to move chairs to shout. The children had to go into the back to provide space for guests. God was truly adding to the church such as should be saved in the "Fish Market Experience".

Now, the pastor, the ministers and the deacons began to look over the city to see what land was available to build a house for the Lord. We looked at the land near Crooms School by Academy

Manor, but that was not it. We also looked at the land on 18th Street. We considered 20th Street and Southwest Road by the railroad tracks. We investigated the building owned by Food Fair on 25th Street and Park Avenue. Many situations were looked into to no avail.

During this period of time, Ingrid shared with me that she and her mother, Mrs. Cleo Burton, owned the property across the street from the "fish market". She asked me to see if Pastor could use it although it seemed small for a church building. When I mentioned it to Pastor, she said, "That's it!" It immediately agreed with her spirit that this was a part of the vision. She said for me to go talk to my wife and her mother and see if they would sell the land and for how much.

Ingrid was happy to hear that the land was suitable. As we considered what to do, Ingrid told me that she wanted her mother to get whatever price she desired. In order for the church to be built faster, Ingrid wanted to donate her part and even considered paying off any liens or taxes so that the church would not have that expense. She asked the Lord to prepare her to offer the land free and clear. She did not want to miss it, desire it or look back in any way. She wanted to be a cheerful giver, and the devil was not going to spoil her sacrifice. To be sure that it was the Lord speaking to us, I decided that we should fast and pray about it. After the fast, we joined hands in prayer and knew in our hearts that God had said, "Yes."

BY MOTHER YVONNE JENKINS

I met Pastor Bryant in 1989. The first time I heard her speak, I knew she was special. The message she preached was 'Pick up the Fragments that none be lost.' It was as though she was preaching only to me. I was going through a rough time. My health had become so bad that I had to quit my job. I had my mentally handicapped daughter and all five of my grandchildren to care for. I was not pleased with the church where I was attending so I joined Tabernacle of Prayer and have not regretted leaving my old church. Pastor Bryant has taught me how to live holy and to lean and depend on Jesus for my very substance. For you see, I was diagnosed with degenerative - rheumatoid arthritis. I could not stand for very long periods of time. Not being able to work, I did not have finances. One Wednesday night during a service, the Lord told me through Pastor Bryant to stop worrying about a job. I had one nurturing my girls. He would send everything we needed to our door. God has been faithful to His word. He said I was blessed, my children were blessed and my home was blessed. I thank God for my leader, one who preaches the truth and lives it as well. **TO GOD BE THE GLORY!**

BY WILMA S. MCDOUGALD

From a very young age, I had been plagued with many infirmities and because my mother had very little money, she did not take me to the doctor very much; therefore, the sickness went unattended. On October 3, I became very ill I began to vomit blood severely. I was taken to the emergency room and diagnosed with an ulcer. I was sent home with a bottle of Maalox but before I could exit the emergency room, the procedure started over again. I was sent to Mercy hospital in Orlando for 10 days. When I came home, my neighbor, who now is my pastor, came over to see me.

I remember the first time I met her after moving into the neighborhood; I was in awe about her voice. She had the softest voice and a sweet attitude. I thought to myself, she must be an angel. Well, Pastor Bryant (Sister Buie at that time) sat by my bed and read scriptures to me. Even though I had gone to church and heard the scriptures read, never had I heard them read the way she did. Not only did she read the scriptures to me, but she prayed that God would heal my body as well. The results were visibly seen. I was able to get up and move about. I thank God for her because had not she been placed in my life, I probably would be dead.

ENDURING FOR THE CAUSE OF CHRIST BY ETHEL BONNER

The Tabernacle Ministry, under the leadership of Pastor Carrie Bryant, means many things to me. It was through many trials and persecutions that I have endured because of standing with this ministry.

I must reflect back to when I first met Pastor Bryant. It was at a local church in which I was a member during the year of 1976. Her laser beaming eyes mesmerized me and appeared to have cut my very soul. The message that she was preaching was on the inner man, 'Though the outward man perishes, the inward man is renewed day by day. I had not heard preaching like that before. I was tired of the familiar Bible stories; my very soul wanted more. I had been crying out to God prior to my first meeting Pastor Bryant. I wanted to be real with my salvation; I wanted to endure and I didn't want to be deceived. Being a part of this ministry has attributed to my still being saved today.

This ministry means deliverance to me because it has and continues to deliver my soul from starvation by filling me up with the proper nourishment of a wholesome diet with the unadulterated word of God. This ministry also means hope to me. Regardless to what state of mind or spirit I was in, while attending service, I was motivated with words of wisdom through the preaching of the Gospel before leaving service. For one needs hope when he / she is unequally joined to an unbeliever in marriage. Two can not walk together unless they agree.

The words, 'you must overcome evil with good,' spoken by my pastor, were the words of hope from God's word that rang out in my hearing whenever my flesh wanted revenge.

This ministry does not compromise with my flesh. Holiness is the standard for God's people, and we are encouraged to live it. I have been accused of many things, which were not true.

During the early stages of the ministry, my self-esteem dropped because of the physical, mental and verbal abuse. My spouse has broken my nose because I came home late from church. I have been dragged from my bedroom to the kitchen and pushed out the door in my nightclothes.

Whenever we had highly anointed services, and the Lord poured out of His spirit, I definitely encountered some blows. The electricity would be turned off from the main switch to prevent me from reading my Bible when I came home from church. My car keys have been taken, my tires slashed, my car tag bent and taken off - all of this to prevent me from worshipping my God. My husband has come to the church to see if I was there or just to see what was happening. Those were embarrassing moments. Out of all my hurt and pain, I am a stronger and better person. This ministry is my life. It is worth all the persecutions that I have endured.

BY RUTHA EVERETT

I met Evangelist Carrie Buie in 1971 at Hickory Avenue Church of God. From the moment I saw her, I knew she would be a great blessing to my spiritual life. I must get to know her, thinking to myself. Her niece and I were friends and she moved into her home. That opened the door for me. Every Sunday I would make my way to her home just to be in her presence.

Evangelist Buie was the musician and choir director at the church. When it came to God's business, she was very serious. She did not condone foolishness. She believed in giving God the best. She had such a sweet, drawing spirit. All the youth loved her and wanted to go to her home.

She became my role model; someone with whom I could talk when things troubled me. She would always give me the word of God. I remembered when she took me to the convention in Jacksonville. It was just her and me, as we rode down the highway, I felt so special to be going with her she'll never know what this did for me.

Evangelist Buie was the person I would call when my hormones began to do their own thing. I would pick up the phone and call her and begin to tell her how I thought I was feeling, so she asked me, "Do you have a boyfriend?" I replied, "No!" In return she commented, "What are you going to do, take someone off the street?" Then she began to minister the word of God to me. I believe the Lord sent her back to Sanford just for me. She has been there for me through the years, both spiritually and naturally.

I remember her going into her closet giving me clothes to wear and food to eat. To this day I have never heard a soul mention this or that. There was nothing I couldn't talk to her about, no hour was too early or too late, it was always the word of the God she preached in my hearing. I can truly say she has been here for me as a teenager, young adult, and now adult. I thank the Lord for Pastor Bryant she has been a jewel in my life and holds a special place in my heart.

BY EVANGELIST SANDRA HAYNES

In 1985 I became a member of the Tabernacle of Prayer in Sanford, Florida. Within a few months the church would be celebrating what was called the "Fifty Day Consecration". On the second night of prayer, the Lord allowed me to be in an anointed prayer service. As I was praying I asked God to save me from every disease of the devil. I remember calling out "Cancer", not knowing that the devil would try to attack my body. When I arrived home that night after prayer, the devil did attacked my body. I went to the doctor I had been going to for over ten years. He detected something abnormal from his examination. He later referred me to a specialist.   The week before seeing the specialist the saints gathered around me and prayed the prayer of faith and I heard the word of the Lord witness within my spirit confirming the scripture. "He was wounded for our transgressions, He was bruised for our iniquities; the chastisement of our peace was upon him and with his stripes we are healed." Isaiah 53:5

I believed in that word with all my heart. This ministry helped increase my faith. From that day until this I have been healed. After seeing the specialist he replied, "I don't see any cancer." To God be the Glory for the things He has done for me. Thanks to you Pastor Bryant for the word of God preached that constantly ministers to my spirit.

Direct contact can be made with the author of the autobiography for speaking invitations, television & radio appearances, and other oratory activities by writing:

Pastor/Presiding Elder Carrie Bryant
Sanford Tabernacle of Prayer Inc.,
P.O. Box 1822
Sanford, Florida
32772-1822
(407)322-4070

or

You may contact the publisher at:
The Great House Publishing(NBN) Inc.,
P.O. Box 574244
Orlando, Florida
32857-4244

ORDER FORM

Quantity	Description	Unit Cost	Total
_____	From Hard To Heart	$24.95	_____
_____	The Destiny Of The Black	$14.95	_____
_____	The Effectual Fervent Prayer	$8.95	_____
_____	The Prophetic Life	$19.95	_____
_____	My Lover's Arms	$19.95	_____
_____	Life Between Seedtime & Harvest	$12.95	_____

Subtotal _____

Discount _____

Taxes(7%) _____

S & H(10%) _____

Total _____

Please make all payments in the form of Money Order or Company Check payable to The Great House Publishing(NBN) Inc. except when otherwise advised by responsible personnel of the company. All outstanding invoices are charged 2% per month or 24% per annum. All returned checks will be charged there appropriate NSF fees and returned items have a charge back of 15% restocking fee.

Address: P.O. Box 574244
Orlando, Florida
32857-4244